Where Angels Fear to Tread

Jack Fitzgerald

Other Jack Fitzgerald books from Creative Book Publishing

Amazing Newfoundland Stories	ISBN 0-920021-36-0	$9.95
Strange But True Newfoundland Stories	ISBN 0-920021-57-3	$9.95
Newfoundland Fireside Stories	ISBN 0-920021-78-6	$9.95
Another Time, Another Place	ISBN 1-895387-75-2	$11.95
The Hangman is Never Late	ISBN 1-894294-02-5	$12.95
Beyond Belief	ISBN 1-894294-31-9	$12.95
Jack Fitzgerald's Notebook	ISBN 1-894294-40-8	$12.95

Ask your favourite bookstore or order directly from the publisher.

Creative Book Publishing
P.O. Box 8660
36 Austin Street
St. John's, NF
A1B 3T7

phone: (709) 722-8500
fax: (709) 579-7745
e-mail: books@rb.nf.ca

Please add $5.00 Canadian for shipping and handling and taxes on single book orders and $1.00 for each additional book.

Where Angels Fear to Tread

Jack Fitzgerald

Creative Publishers
St. John's, Newfoundland
1995

©1995 Jack Fitzgerald

Le Conseil des Arts du Canada | The Canada Council for the Arts

We acknowledge the support of The Canada Council for the Arts for our publishing program.

We acknowledge the financial support of the Government of Canada through the Book Publishing Industry Development Program (BPIDP) for our publishing program.

All rights reserved. No part of this work covered by the copyrights hereon may be reproduced or used in any form or by any means—graphic, electronic or mechanical—without the prior written permission of the publisher. Any requests for photocopying, recording, taping or information storage and retrieval systems of any part of this book shall be directed in writing to the Canadian Reprography Collective, One Yonge Street, Suite 1900, Toronto, Ontario M5E 1E5.

∞ Printed on acid-free paper

Published by
CREATIVE BOOK PUBLISHING
a division of 10366 Newfoundland Limited
a Robinson-Blackmore Printing & Publishing associated company
P.O. Box 8660, St. John's, Newfoundland A1B 3T7

Second Printing — March 2002

Printed in Canada by:
ROBINSON-BLACKMORE PRINTING & PUBLISHING

National Library of Canada Cataloguing in Publication Data

Fitzgerald, Jack, 1945-
    Where angels fear to tread

    ISBN 1-895387-49-3

    1. Murder — Newfoundland. 2. Trials (Murder) — Newfoundland. 3. Criminal Justice, Administration of — Newfoundland. I. Title

HV6535.C32N488   1995   364.1'523'09718
C95-950086-3

*Dedicated to
Harry, Olivia and their son
Nicholas*

Contents

Chapter 1. A Cause Lost
— *The Brian Smith Story* _ _ _ _ _   1

Chapter 2. The Sand Pits Mystery _ _ _ _ _ _ _ 75

Chapter 3. Newfoundland Connections
— *Foiled Kidnapping* _ _ _ _ _ _ _ 97
— *It Shocked New York* _ _ _ _ _ 100

Chapter 4. The Murder of Mona Johnson _ _ _ 103

Chapter 5. Old Time Justice
— *Attacked with an Axe* _ _ _ _ _ 123
— *The Brawl on McNeil Street* _ _ _ 127
— *A Smart Lawyer* _ _ _ _ _ _ _ 129

Chapter 6. The Wheel of Fortune Spins _ _ _ 131

A CAUSE LOST

THE BRIAN SMITH STORY

BRIAN SMITH, convicted of second degree murder in the shotgun slaying of Jerome Fleming at Bay Bulls on April 5, 1984, went to his grave insisting he was innocent. Smith and Fleming were best friends.

During his trial Smith took the stand to testify. He claimed his innocence and told the court he had already spent a year in jail for a crime he did not commit.

The jury weighed the evidence given at the trial and convicted Smith of second degree murder. Judge Gerald Lang sentenced him to twenty years in prison, with a minimum of ten years to be served before parole eligibility.

Throughout his prison term Smith always maintained his innocence. In 1990 his plight drew media attention when *The Sunday Express* published a three-part series on his case. Later the CBC aired a documentary on Smith's effort to clear his name.

Smith claimed that RCMP officers had lied and twisted his comments to give a meaning opposite to what was intended. During the trial Sergeant Douglas Hamlyn testified that Smith verbally admitted killing Fleming, while Smith's written statement claimed innocence.

In a voir dire, lasting four days, Smith's lawyer argued to prevent the police officer from giving that evidence in court. The police officer claimed that Smith made self-incriminating statements to him while he was being held at the Ferryland RCMP offices. Judge Lang ruled that the police evidence was admissible. He said he was satisfied that Smith's statements were voluntary and that he had been given the police caution.

Smith was not a credible witness on the stand. His testimony often conflicted with that given by other witnesses close to him, including his wife. His lawyer at the trial, Ernest Gittens, in an interview with the *Sunday Express* on September 9, 1990, expressed regret in having placed Smith on the stand. He was quoted as saying, "He came across terribly evasive and certainly not believable. My heart sort of sank."

In 1990 Smith launched a public campaign to clear his name and win release from prison. However, just as his efforts were reaching a peak, personal tragedy struck. Doctors told him that he had terminal cancer.

Jerome Kennedy, Smith's lawyer at that time, successfully had him moved to a hospital at St. John's so he could be near his family. Soon after, with his condition worsening, the appeal court allowed him to go free on bail. Then, on February 3, 1994, Brian Smith passed away. His appeal died with him. He died insisting he was an innocent man.

Brian Smith's encounter with the justice system had its beginning in a forested area overlooking the scenic harbour at Bay Bulls. During the early part of April, 1984, Bay Bulls was covered in a blanket of snow. Roads were narrowed by snow banks and cool temperatures prevailed. Alphonse Mulcahey, a resident of Bay Bulls was in the habit of taking a daily walk along the Quay's Road on the southside of the community. Mulcahey knew the people in the area and they knew him. These walks were usually quiet and uneventful except for the odd passing car or a neighbour shouting a greeting.

His walk on the afternoon of April 7 was to be different. His discovery would soon bring police cars with sirens blasting and flashing lights to this ordinarily quiet road. A pile of debris about forty or fifty feet off the road caught his eye. He had not noticed this in his walks earlier that week. Mulcahey could see a green car seat, some pop bottles and some beer bottles which looked like they were unopened.

Mulcahey's first impression was that someone had thrown garbage in the woods, and he moved into the area to have a closer look. Near the seat he saw a man's body lying motionless in the winter snow. "I immediately checked for a pulse and when I found none I left to call the RCMP," Mulcahey later recalled.

Constable John Campbell of the Ferryland detachment of the RCMP responded to Mulcahey's call. Within minutes other police officers began arriving. Police immediately suspected foul play. Sergeant Doug Hamlyn, quickly took control of the situation; he ordered police to bar off the Quay's Road and he placed Constable John Campbell in charge of gathering the evidence from the scene. Campbell took possession of the car seat, pop bottles, beer bottles and other items left at the site.

Sergeant Hamlyn arranged for a temporary police headquarters to be set up at the elementary school in Bay Bulls to co-ordinate the investigation.

Meanwhile, police were still trying to determine the identity of the victim. The body had been placed in a body bag and moved to the shoulder of the road. Police officers asked three residents of the area — Jack Crane, Angus O'Brien and Alphonsus Mulcahey — to look at the victim to see if he could be identified. However, the man in the body bag was unknown to them.

While the police investigated the area and gathered evidence, Pius Ryan, an undertaker with Ryan's Funeral Home, arrived. Pius recognized the dead man. Joe Ryan, also from Ryan's Funeral Home, confirmed the identification. It was thirty-one-year-old Jerome Fleming. Fleming was not from the area, but Joe Ryan was able to tell police that the victim was a friend of Brian Smith who lived on the north side of Bay Bulls Harbour.

The concentration of police and flashing lights on the police cars parked on the Quay's Road, attracted much attention among the residents of Bay Bulls. Brian Smith received a call from his mother who told him that the police were over on the Quay's Road and suggested something must be wrong over there. Smith took his binoculars and went outside his home to look at the activity across the harbour. Before the night was over the police investigation would be right on his doorstep.

A few hours later the police were knocking on Brian Smith's door. Police records show that Sergeant Doug Hamlyn, head of the RCMP Ferryland Detachment, and Sergeant Harold Avery of the RCMP's General Investigation Section arrived at Smith's at exactly 11:48 p.m. At this time Brian Smith was not a suspect; the police were simply gathering information on Jerome Fleming, and tracing his whereabouts over recent days.

Sergeant Hamlyn recalled that, "We knocked on the door. Mrs. Smith answered and said Brian was not home." However, Brian was home and when he heard his wife talking with the police he came to the door and invited them inside. The two police sergeants and Smith sat at the kitchen table while Patricia Smith went to another area of the house. They did not tell the Smiths that Fleming was dead.

Sergeant Hamlyn explained to Brian that they were checking the whereabouts of Jerome Fleming and they had been told ". . . that Smith was a friend of Fleming." Brian told the police he had last seen Jerome on the evening of Thursday, April 5. He went on to describe the activities of that day and night. Smith told the police he and Jerome were out drinking in Jerome's black Chevette at about 10 p.m. on Thursday night. The police did not take notes during Smith's first recounting of events of April 5.

However, Brian had mentioned several things which

interested them and they went over the whole story a second time. This time they took notes. What seemed to be several minor inconsistencies became, over subsequent days, a pattern which caused police to suspect that Brian Smith had something to hide.

Throughout the first recounting of events of the night of April 5, Brian neglected to mention a van. In recounting the events the first time he told police that he and Fleming had been drinking in a black Chevette owned by Fleming, near his house at 10:00 p.m. He even described the car as having a red interior. During the second recounting of his story he told police Randy Dalton had driven Fleming's black Chevette to St. John's at 9:00 p.m.

When Sergeant Hamlyn mentioned this contradiction to Smith, he replied, "No, I meant the van." Smith offered no explanation of this contradiction. It was the first mention of the van by Smith.

According to Hamlyn's notes of that night, Smith went on to say that "when they were drinking in the van a Gulliver's Cab came along and Jerome had said 'there's my run out;' meaning that was his run out to town that night."

Hamlyn continued: "Smith said a cab came along and parked in front of him. Parked in front of his house and the cab was parked too close to his fence to get the door opened on the passenger side. So the two occupants got out on the drivers' side. Smith noticed the cab light shining on this fellow's bald head or high hairline."

Once again Smith began to backtrack. He told police, ". . . it looked like Dan Coady." The police zeroed in on this to get details to help in their investigation. Sergeant Hamlyn asked Smith for more information on the cab and the visitors. Hamlyn noted, "Smith said the two men came over and got in the van with Jerome. He, Mr. Smith, got out and went into his residence.

"We questioned him about the car and the occupants and he told us it was not a Gulliver's Cab. As a matter of fact it was not a cab at all. It was just a similar colour. No taxi plates on the top or on the back. Not a cab at all. It was a car similar to Gulliver's and he went on to mention Dan Coady. He said it looked like Dan Coady and from there he said it definitely was not Dan Coady."

The conversation with Smith continued and so did the inconsistencies. Smith had indicated that when the two strangers got in the van he left and went into his house. According to Smith that was about 11:30 p.m. During the early part of the questioning Smith said he heard the van leave but did not hear it return. He then went on to say that he went down to the van at about 1:30 a.m. to bring a blanket to Jerome and to pick up two soft drinks and a candy bar he purchased earlier that night for his wife. Smith told the police Jerome was not there and the items he wanted were gone. However, the keys were in the ignition.

Smith explained that he brought the blanket to the van because he did not know if Jerome was going to sleep in the van or go into the house. Police wondered why Jerome would be staying out in the van. It was a cool night. Jerome was Smith's best friend and had slept in the house several times previously, according to Smith.

Another inconsistency in Smith's story which later took on some significance occurred when police focused their questioning on the van. In response to Hamlyn's question about the ownership of the van, Smith answered that it was Jerome's. He added that Jerome had bought it on Wednesday (the day before he was killed) from Pat Murphy of Witless Bay for $120.00. The contradiction involved Smith's explanation of how the van ended up in the possession of Fred Power the day after Fleming's death.

Earlier in the questioning Smith had claimed that he had given the van to Fred Power because Jerome had asked him to sell it. Now he claimed that Fred Power had picked up the van Friday morning (April 6) but he (Brian) had not seen Fred when he came for the van. He said he had assumed that Fred had made arrangements with Jerome to buy the van.

The attention of the investigators now turned to the present location of the van. They asked Smith where they could find it and he gave them Power's telephone number and address. Power lived on the Alley Road at Bay Bulls not too far from the Smith home.

There was nothing unusual in Smith's behaviour during this first encounter with the police. Sergeant Hamlyn recalled, "I did not notice anything about him. He was polite, I suppose normal. I don't know if that's the right word to say or not. But there was nothing unusual about him that evening at all."

Commenting on Smith's reaction to the police presence in his home Hamlyn noted, "Smith had no apparent objection to our being there." He continued, "We had not told him that Fleming was dead, we just told him we were checking his whereabouts during the week. He was talking freely to us."

Just as the police were leaving, Hamlyn informed the Smiths that Jerome Fleming was dead. They showed no reaction to the information. When police left the Smith home at 1:40 a.m., April 8, Brian Smith was not a suspect in the murder. The interview had lasted almost two hours and police had recorded five and a half pages of notes on information given by Smith.

The investigators then went to the home of Fred Power on the Alley Road. Jerome Fleming's van, a 1972 red and black Dodge, was in the driveway. Sergeant Hamlyn began a visual inspection of the van using his flashlight.

The first important lead in the investigation was uncovered by Hamlyn. When he opened the passenger door he noticed, "what I felt or what looked to me to be a piece of flesh on the door post." Behind the passenger seat were several spots which he suspected were blood. Hamlyn closed the van door and called Constable John Campbell to the scene. Campbell arrived at 3:00 a.m., and had the vehicle impounded as evidence. It was towed to the

Ferryland Detachment for a thorough search and investigation.

Early next morning (Monday, April 9) the investigating team met at the temporary headquarters at the Bay Bulls Elementary School. At this early stage in the investigation police were considering four suspects: Randy Dalton, Fred Power, Patricia Smith and Brian Smith.

Because it seemed evident that Fleming had been killed inside the van police wanted to talk again with Brian Smith. He was the last person seen with Fleming in the van on the night of the murder. Hamlyn and Avery arrived at Smith's door at 11:33 a.m. Patricia Smith answered the door and invited them inside. A short while later Brian Smith came out of a bedroom. He was not as co-operative as he had been the night before. Smith made it plain that he did not want to speak with police. Earlier that day he had speculated to a couple of people that he felt the police would try and pin him with Fleming's death.

Sergeant Hamlyn took notes of what transpired that day. He noted, "I told him that Corporal Hogg and Constable Ryan were coming for him. Smith said he called his lawyer this morning and has an appointment for 12 o'clock tomorrow." Smith told Hamlyn that he did not want to talk with the police.

Hamlyn recalled, "Smith said he did not want to incriminate anyone or anybody. He said there are a lot of things on the go; armed robberies and that, and he had received a lot of calls on this. He said, 'Its hard to explain what happened to your buddy.' At this point Smith turned to his wife and asked her to call Roland." Sergeant Hamlyn knew that Smith was referring to his lawyer Roland Snelgrove. Following a short conversation between Smith and Snelgrove on the phone Smith said he did not want to talk to anybody else.

However, Hamlyn was not allowing himself to be brushed aside that easily. The Sergeant said, "I told Mr. Smith we needed to talk to him again and that we were going to talk to him and that we did not want to arrest him. But if we had to we would."

Smith was reluctant to go. He expressed concern about leaving his wife without wood to keep the fire going. It was a cold day and along with the need for heat she needed the stove going to cook for the family. Hamlyn told Smith that he and Sergeant Avery would take care of that and he need not worry. Smith replied, "I'll go with you." He got ready, went to the bathroom, and then was taken to police offices at Ferryland by Hogg and Ryan.

At Ferryland, Corporal Hogg read Smith his rights. Then the interrogation began. It lasted nine hours with a one hour break for supper. For the first two hours police concentrated their questioning on the events of Thursday, April 5, and Smith's relationship with the victim.

The suspect described Fleming's last hours. He told police he had last seen Jerome on the evening of April 5 when they were together drinking in Jerome's van. The van was parked outside Smith's house. Smith said a light coloured car pulled in front of the van. Fleming indicated the men were taking him to St. John's. Smith said he got out of the van and walked up to his house. It was dark and the area was poorly lit. Smith did not get a good look at the two visitors.

His statement claimed that at about 2:00 a.m. he went out to the van to give Fleming a blanket, but Fleming was not in the van. During the lengthy interrogation Smith also told police that Fleming and Randy Dalton were at his house on April 5. He explained that he had an arrangement with the two to pay them to cut sticks which he used to repair his home and build a verandah.

He had agreed to pay one dollar per stick, or the equivalent in marijuana.

In his statement to police, Smith also admitted to dealing in drugs in the Bay Bulls area. Fleming, according to Smith, was not a big player in the drug trade. He said, "He (Fleming) only sold five and ten dollar lots of marijuana." Smith also told police he had heard that

Fleming had been shot by a bullet fired through the seat of the van to muffle the sound.

Constable Ryan asked Smith if he was aware of anyone having a grudge against Fleming. Smith replied, "If anyone had a grudge against Fleming they would have one against me too."

Police then focused on the question of who killed Jerome Fleming. Smith offered several possibilities. He suggested the name of Peter Gulliver, a taxi driver, with whom Fleming was having trouble. Also, he suggested that Fleming did not get along with his sister's husband.

Ryan asked Smith if he knew of any motive for killing Fleming. The suspect answered that he couldn't think of any. He added, "Fleming was a decent guy and no one would want to hurt him." Smith broke down and cried at this point. The questioning went on until 10:30 p.m. After comparing Smith's statement with other evidence gathered to date, the police decided to arrest Brian Smith on a charge of first degree murder.

While the police interrogated Brian Smith at Ferryland, his wife Patricia and Freddy Power were being questioned at RCMP offices in St. John's. In a 1990 interview with the *Sunday Express* Mrs. Smith claimed, "They told me that they had Brian in the other room just up the hall." Freddy Power also said that he was told by police officers that Brian was just down the hall.

The *Express* article quoted Mrs. Smith: "Sergeant Hamlyn sat up in front of me and told me that Brian confessed to killing Jerome and that as far as he was concerned, I was involved in it too."

She added, "He said, that as far as he was concerned, I helped Brian dispose of the body and he told me that I could lose my kids if I did not tell the truth. He really scared me. They told me that everything I said in my statement was a lie." Sergeant Hamlyn denied at the trial that he ever threatened Mrs. Smith. Mrs. Smith said she broke down and cried. She said she told Sergeant Hamlyn that she did not believe Brian had confessed.

During his confinement at Ferryland, Smith had a series of encounters with Sergeant Doug Hamlyn which became controversial at the trial. These sessions and what was discussed became an important part of Smith's trial, and, over recent years, central to his claim of innocence. According to Hamlyn, Smith talked as if he had killed Fleming, but denied having done so throughout. Finally, Hamlyn's notes record: Smith verbally admitted to killing Jerome Fleming.

Sergeant Hamlyn knew on the night of Monday, April 9, that he would be talking to Brian Smith the next day. Smith was due to be charged in provincial court at Ferryland the next morning. Hamlyn had been in charge of the Ferryland Detachment for two and a half years and was in the habit of arriving for work between 6:00 a.m. and 6:30 a.m. He arrived for work on April 10 at 6:20 a.m. Smith was in his cell and awake when Sergeant Hamlyn arrived. The sergeant invited Smith to come outside his cell for a cup of coffee. Smith agreed but told Hamlyn he didn't like coffee and asked for tea instead. Smith, Hamlyn and Constable Baker sat at a table in the interrogating room.

"You need not say anything," Hamlyn began reading the police caution from a card. "You have nothing to hope from any promise or favour and nothing to fear from any threat, whether or not you say anything. Anything you do say, may be used as evidence." Smith was apparently nervous. He was rubbing his hands together and rubbing them through his hair. When Hamlyn asked him if he understood the caution Smith answered that he did. He commented that he had been given the caution, "yesterday by the other police officers." Smith did not ask to consult with a lawyer and he did not object to the questioning that followed.

"I told Smith I was investigating the death of Jerome Fleming and I was satisfied that he was responsible," said Hamlyn. The discussion at first was in general about Smith's situation. Hamlyn recalled, "He wanted to know if he was going to be charged. I told him he was to be charged with first degree murder. He wanted to know when he was going to court. I told him today. He wanted to know if he was going to St. John's. I told him no. It would be in Ferryland."

Before being taken over to Court to be charged, Smith talked with his lawyer by telephone. Mr. Snelgrove advised Smith that he should seek another lawyer with experience in handling a murder trial. He recommended John McGrath.

Sergeant Hamlyn asked Smith to tell him about Fleming. The accused replied that he could not because the caution was in the way. He did, however, tell the two police officers that he did not have any reason to kill Jerome Fleming.

"I told him I felt the death was accidental," said Hamlyn, "possibly he could have cleared the whole matter up if he had reported it at the time to the police. I asked him if they were planning an armed robbery and the gun went off in the van. He stated he was not into armed robberies. We talked more about how the death may have come about if the gun discharged accidentally. He stated he could not talk about it because he knew nothing about it and stated he had an appointment with his lawyer at 12:00 noon and after that he would talk to me if his lawyer advised him."

Sergeant Hamlyn added, "I told him I could understand why he would dump the body. If this was accidental or any other way he would panic and get rid of it." Smith's reply was, "There is no explanation for dumping your best friend in the woods."

Smith's reaction to the question suggested to Hamlyn that Smith might prefer to talk with him one-on-one. Hamlyn knew Smith previously to this murder investigation; he had talked with him before about another criminal matter and he felt he got along well with the accused. The sergeant asked Baker to get more coffee and when he returned suggested to him that he wait outside.

Describing the mood in the interrogating room that morning, Sergeant Hamlyn recalled, "I felt Smith wanted to talk to me. He obviously wanted to talk to somebody. Not by any words he said, but I had the impression he might feel better about talking to one member alone, and that it was me. I had talked to Smith before. We got along well. So because of that he did not ask for Baker to leave. That was my idea."

Although a congenial mood existed between the two adversaries, Sergeant Hamlyn never lost sight of his investigative goals. He was certain Brian Smith had pulled the trigger, and now he was attempting to get the full story and gain an admission of guilt.

Once again Hamlyn raised the possibility of accidental death. He said, "I told him there was a possibility he could get out of this fairly easily if this death was accidental, and he stated there is no way of walking out of this. Accidental death means three years. He said he's better off taking his chances on the murder charge. He might not be convicted."

Hamlyn continued, "He stated he would take his chances with the murder charge. He said he would talk to his lawyer and would see if he could work out a deal. He made a statement that he could not tell me anything because the caution was there. This was the only time I said to him to forget the caution, as if it were not there." When Hamlyn attempted to continue on with the discussion Smith said he had no knowledge or involvement in the killing. He said he felt sorry for his [Smith's] family.

It seemed, however, as the questioning went on that Smith let his guard down on several occasions. Sergeant Hamlyn recalled that Smith had been talking about the crime as though he had committed it, but then would correct himself and deny involvement. During a discussion on the gun, Sergeant Hamlyn said, "I asked him if the whole thing could be straightened out if he could turn the gun over to me?"

"You told me the gun was not yours. Was it Jerome's?" asked Sergeant Hamlyn.

"Yes, b'y," answered Smith.

"Did you bring the gun into the van?" asked Hamlyn.

"No, I did not," replied Smith.

Hamlyn recalled, "I asked him when Jerome brought it in the van and he told me he did not see Jerome bringing it in the van. I asked him if the gun was in the van when he got in the van and he said that is right. I asked him what he did with the gun. Did you hide it or throw it away? He said I cannot tell you that but you will never find it." Hamlyn added, "Smith then went on to say that he did not mean to say that. What he meant was if he had done it the gun would not be available."

According to Hamlyn, Smith commented, "John McGrath (Smith's lawyer) is ready to hang me now for talking to you too much already. I said, 'You tell John McGrath that you got him hired and that you can fire him if you want to.' He said 'That is right. I can fire him. Maybe I will get another lawyer. Perhaps Gerry O'Brien tomorrow morning.' We both had a good laugh about changing lawyers."

According to Sergeant Hamlyn, throughout the one-on-one conversation, "He was reacting favourable. We were getting along." The police sergeant noted that although Smith showed no reluctance to participate in the questioning he was often, "guarded in his conversation."

During the fingerprinting process later that morning Smith observed Sergeant Hamlyn at his desk writing notes. When the fingerprinting was finished Smith asked Hamlyn why he was taking notes. The veteran investigator explained, "I have to make notes of conversations every time we talk." Smith told the sergeant that he (Smith) had not made any notes so far, but that he was going to start.

Sergeant Hamlyn permitted Smith to use his office in private to make a call to McGrath. Hamlyn remained outside the office but could see Smith through a window.

The investigator noted, "When he came out he said he had nothing further to say. He asked for pen and paper and that he be put in a place alone so he could take notes of what had happened so far." The police gave Smith pen and paper and returned him to his cell.

When Smith appeared in court that day he was remanded for three days by Magistrate Terry Corbett. The judge also ordered that he see a doctor. Smith discussed this with his lawyer by telephone and was told to talk with no one. McGrath said that he would meet with him in St. John's later that week.

Later that day Smith refused to speak with either Dr. Peter Morey or Father Kevin Molloy. However, he reconsidered his decision not to speak with Father Molloy and agreed to talk with him the next day. Smith had a deep respect for Father Molloy. Father Molloy had christened Smith's first child and Smith had waited two months so he could have Father Molloy christen his second child. Police notes indicated that Father Molloy was also respected on the Southern Shore for his expertise on the Narcotics Control Act.

Smith told Sergeant Hamlyn he intended to speak with Father Molloy and suggested he might wish to speak with the sergeant after the meeting. Hamlyn advised Smith to discuss the question of accidental death with the priest and talk to him afterwards.

The investigator noted, "He said he might want to talk to me again and [asked] if it could be put off until Friday. I told him that was up to him — I would talk to him anytime. I would prefer to talk to him before."

At another point while Smith was at Ferryland, Sergeant Hamlyn discussed the meaning of the police caution with Smith. Responding to Hamlyn's question about the caution, Smith replied that he understood its meaning. Hamlyn asked him to explain it in his own words. Smith answered, "It means you have the right to counsel. You have the right to remain silent and anything you say can be used in court."

"Then you understand the police caution," commented Hamlyn.

"Yes, I do, and I got nothing to say if you're going to be asking any questions. You cautioned me the other day."

The most contentious point in the police evidence occurred on the morning of April 12. According to Sergeant Hamlyn, Smith admitted to the crime during a one-on-one conversation with him. Hamlyn noted that Smith was pessimistic over his chances in court. "He said he didn't have a chance in court, and if he testified the crown prosecutor would tear him apart." Just after saying this, according to Hamlyn, Smith commented, "I did it, but I have to take my chances." Hamlyn added that Smith indicated he would like to serve his term at Kingston prison.

On April 12, when alone with Hamlyn, Smith asked, "What would happen if I went all the way and changed my plea to guilty on the last day, would the charge be reduced from first degree murder?"

"I could not comment on that," replied Sergeant Hamlyn. Instead, he suggested that Smith discuss that with his lawyer. Hamlyn added, "After that we talked about his knowledge of the offence. I asked him what he would expect to get for a sentence if he took the stand in court and told what really happened because he is the only one who could really do that."

The sergeant continued, "Smith said 'If I told the nitty gritty details, I would expect to get ten years. There's no point in me telling you I did not do it. Because you know the difference.' I said 'That is right. There is a lot of evidence on this.' "

According to Hamlyn, Smith replied, " 'Well, if a person found himself in the position I am in and told the details he would likely get five to ten years.' He then asked me what is meant by manslaughter. I explained to him that is a situation where one person causes the death of another with some carelessness involved but no planning to kill the other person."

Sergeant Hamlyn then suggested that the killing was likely related to a drug deal. He said, "The gun was in the car." Smith interjected, "The van."

Hamlyn said, "OK, something went wrong." Smith commented, "It was not even my gun."

Hamlyn said, "I expect it was Fleming's gun. I asked who took the gun into the van and he told me he did not take it in. I asked him what he did with the gun after."

Smith replied, "I am not saying I had a gun."

The conversation then turned to Smith's drug dealings. The police sergeant told Smith that he was aware that Smith had purchased a pound of marijuana on April 5 the day Fleming was killed. Smith replied that Fleming had nothing to do with that deal. He admitted to having the drugs but explained that he had sold it around Bay Bulls. Smith told Hamlyn he couldn't give him the names of those who purchased the marijuana.

Hamlyn noted that Smith enjoyed talking about the drugs. They both laughed and shared a few jokes. Hamlyn said, "Smith said he sold drugs at the Sou'wester Lounge in the Gould's and did a good business. He said I would be surprised if I knew some of the people he was selling drugs to. One was a high government official."

The topic then changed to Smith's scheduled court appearance for the next day. He was concerned about it and asked if Jerome's family would be there. Sergeant Hamlyn answered that, "It would be reasonable to expect someone from the Fleming family would be in the court." Smith wondered how he should react if the Fleming family was present.

The police sergeant asked, "What do you do? Do you talk to them? Do you apologize or do you just walk by them, ignore them."

Smith answered that he did not know what he would do. He added, "I will walk straight ahead. Look straight ahead and not talk to anybody."

The following morning when Sergeant Hamlyn arrived for work he went to Smith's cell and said, "Rise and shine, we are going for a drive this morning." He invited Smith to have a cup of tea with him and Smith replied, "Yes, by!" The prisoner was to be taken to St. John's later that day to enter his plea on a charge of first degree murder.

Meanwhile, Hamlyn was most attentive to anything Smith might say which could be used as evidence or in someway help with the investigation. Hamlyn recalled, "I asked him if he understood he is still under caution and he said yes and he got nothing to say. I told him I would like to come into the cell and talk to him. I said we could talk about the weather if he wanted to. He said OK."

When the tea was brought to Smith in a styrofoam cup, Sergeant Hamlyn commented, "These cups are no good for hot drinks. I'll get some real cups." Smith agreed and minutes later the two were immersed in conversation.

The police sergeant noted that Smith was not cautioned and there was no threat. Brian Smith's thoughts that morning were with his family. "Smith was wondering what he would tell his wife," said Hamlyn. "He was talking about moving his wife and family to the mainland and he said he would tell his wife he was innocent whether he was innocent or not," added Hamlyn.

He continued, "I told him that in my opinion his wife was the one person who deserved to know the truth about it. Then we talked about what would happen in court. He wanted to get a remand to the Waterford Hospital. Accommodations there, according to Smith, were much better than at the Pen. I told him I had no control over that. I told him I would tell the crown prosecutor what he wanted but the decision on what would happen would be made by the judge. We had no control over it whatever." At the Court House in St. John's Smith met with his lawyer, John McGrath, and held a conversation with his wife. When he appeared in court he was remanded again until April 24.

Meanwhile, the police were conducting an intensive

investigation in the Bay Bulls area. Several searches were made at the Smith residence. An RCMP diving team searched the Bay Bulls harbour and police plodded through a door-to-door questioning of people in the community.

Corporal Tom Bennett of the Holyrood RCMP detachment was in command of the St. John's Sub-Division Diving Team. Bennett's men searched the harbour for a week. They began in the waters near where the victim was found on the south side of the bay. The two-day effort there failed to turn up any evidence. However, they were more fortunate when they moved to the area near Smith's house on the north side.

On April 16 the divers were searching the waters near Smith's home on the north side of Bay Bulls. Near Maloney's wharf, across from Smith's house, the divers found parts of a shotgun barrel and sixteen live shotgun shells. A little further down the shore two young boys found a gun stock which had washed ashore. Somebody had gone through a lot of trouble to dispose of the murder weapon. The barrel had been sawed off and sawed down the middle. The gun stock was also sawed off and the pieces tossed into the waters of Bay Bulls harbour.

In addition to the gun, someone had tossed a box of cartridges into the water.

Suspecting that Smith may have cut the gun up in his house, the police searched the home and removed multiple items for examination. They confiscated saws, an axe, a piece of the carpeting and some clothing. This evidence was sent to the RCMP lab at New Brunswick for examination. The police felt they had a major breakthrough in the investigation.

Sergeant Hamlyn was pleased with the progress. He commented, "I had reason to believe this was the gun used in the death of Fleming." In addition, investigation had found an expended cartridge near where the victim was found, as well as metal filings found in the Smith home. After considering the evidence gathered so far, Hamlyn decided it was time to talk with Smith again.

This time the meeting took place in a large room at Her Majesty's Penitentiary. The only furniture there consisted of a small green table and four chairs. It was August 19, two weeks after the death of Jerome Fleming.

Hamlyn started the conversation by giving the police caution. Once again it was a one-on-one interview. He told Smith of the recent developments in the investigation. Hamlyn told Smith that he felt certain when the lab reports were finished they would confirm the gun had been filed down in Smith's house and it was the gun used to kill Fleming. The conversation did not last long.

Smith responded, suggesting that the evidence police had was circumstantial, and there was no proof that he had pulled the trigger. The accused suggested that Jerome Fleming could have accidently shot himself. Sergeant Hamlyn countered that the situation did not appear that way, because of the way the incident had been covered up.

Smith's attitude had changed from earlier meetings with Hamlyn. "There was no smiling, no laughing," said Hamlyn, "On that day he was not at all pleasant to me."

Hamlyn noted, "Smith said the lawyer was ready to hang him for even sitting there with me. He said he had nothing else to say. He was going for a long time. His wife knows nothing about it. He hoped we would keep him here so he could see the family. He said he got nothing further to say. He got up and walked out of the room." It was 9:27 a.m.

Describing Smith's mood that morning Sergeant Hamlyn stated, "He was quite serious about the situation. He appeared at the time to have a dislike for me. If I can say it that strongly. My feeling was confirmed when he walked out and left me there."

On January 21, 1985, the first degree murder trial of Brian Smith got underway in the Supreme Court of Newfoundland at St. John's. A jury of six men and six women was chosen. The presiding Judge was Justice Gerald Lang. Acting for the Crown was a veteran prosecutor, John Byrne. Meanwhile, by trial date Smith had switched lawyers for the third time. He replaced John McGrath with Ernest Gittins. Smith explained that he had problems with McGrath because he also handled the mortgage on Smith's house at Bay Bulls.

The RCMP had conducted a comprehensive investigation and the Crown went into the trial well prepared. Sergeant Hamlyn's evidence of Smith admitting to the killing was an important part of the case. However, it was not the only significant evidence. John Byrne pieced together a chain of circumstances from which he hoped to persuade the jury that the only conclusion to be drawn was that Brian Smith killed Jerome Fleming.

The first prosecution witness was Corporal Patrick Laturnus, from the RCMP identification section. He described for the court the items recovered from the murder scene. These included beer bottles, soft drink bottles, expended shotgun shells, a car seat and a paper bag containing a chocolate bar wrapper.

Laturnus testified that he failed to find any fingerprints on the bottles or the chocolate bar. He explained that the damp weather may have washed the fingerprints away. The witness also searched the van for fingerprints but found none.

The next crown witness described the finding of the murder weapon. Constable Joseph St. Laurent told the court that the gun recovered was the one believed used to kill Fleming. The gun had been recovered from the waters in the area of Bay Bulls harbour near the Smith residence.

Under cross-examination by Mr. Gittens, St. Laurent admitted, "The discovery of the shotgun was considered a major breakthrough." He added, "But [it was] only one part of important evidence gathered."

A snow storm struck the Avalon Peninsula on the morning of January 29, 1985, forcing Judge Lang to postpone the trial. The first week of the trial had been taken up with the presentation of exhibits — including photographs — into the evidence.

When the trial resumed the defence attempted to block the evidence of Sergeant Hamlyn, who claimed that Smith had confessed to the killing.

To decide on the issue, Judge Lang convened a Voir Dire (legal term for a trial within a trial to determine admissibility of evidence and settle disputed legal arguments). When a Voir Dire is conducted the jury is asked to leave the courtroom so they will not be influenced by the evidence and legal arguments presented.

In this Voir Dire, Judge Lang wanted to determine the answer to two questions. First, were the statements made voluntarily? Second, was Smith given the police caution before the questioning?

During the Voir Dire, the repeated references by Sergeant Hamlyn to notes he recorded during his conversations with the accused became a source of controversy. At times, Hamlyn gave the impression that he had no actual memory of certain events other than what he had recorded in his notes. This practice irritated defence counsel Gittens who put forward a series of objections to the practice.

The first in a series of incriminating statements was made by Smith during a forty minute period between 6:30 and 7:10 a.m. the morning after his arrest in a one-on-one conversation with Sergeant Hamlyn. The police officer told the court that he did not take notes during the session. He waited until breakfast was brought in at 8:38. He then left the room and made notes of the conversation at that time. An hour and forty minutes had elapsed and Gittens questioned whether Hamlyn's recollections were comprehensive enough to give the court a clear and accurate picture of the conversation.

Mr. Gittens asked, "Did you have any difficulty in remembering the words of the accused? This was 8:38 and your conversation took place 6:30 to 7:10 a.m."

Sergeant Hamlyn testified, "I noted what I remembered. I noted what I considered to be admissions on his part and what I considered to be denials. I do know that I cautioned him and the gist of what we talked about is noted. In some cases the particular words are noted — like what I considered to be admissions and denials are noted. He might have said the same thing three or four times. I might not have noted it three or four times but it is noted."

Sergeant Hamlyn described the circumstances surrounding the one-on-one conversation with Smith the morning after he was arrested. He told the court he had several times raised the possibility to Smith that the death had been accidental. The witness stated, "Smith was nervous about the accidental part because accidental meant three years and he felt he would be better off taking his chances on the murder charge. He said he might not be convicted."

He added, "I said whatever he told me I would have to tell the prosecutor and he said he understood that. However, he couldn't tell me if it was accidental or anything else. He left it at that." On several occasions Sergeant Hamlyn referred to his notes before answering questions.

Mr. Gittens again objected to the police officer's frequent references to his notes. He addressed the judge saying, "I would take exception to the procedure being adopted by this witness in relation to his frantically looking for something in his notes to read off to the court. If he has a recollection of it and it is not a specific item, a date, a time or a place — he is being asked what his response is to a particular event?"

Judge Lang: "Yes."

Mr. Gittens: "If he has a recollection of that he should give it to the court. Otherwise, if he is going to go to his notes then I will submit to the court that what he is doing is reading from his notes."

Prosecutor, John Byrne, defended Hamlyn's use of his

notes. He asked, "What is the purpose of having the notes for the purpose of refreshing your memory if you are not going to refer to them?"

The Judge permitted Hamlyn to refer to his notes.

Sergeant Hamlyn referred to the first conversation he held with Smith. He told the court, "I asked him again if he would tell me about it and clear the matter up. He said he could not because the caution was in the way."

Mr. Byrne interjected, "So, he indicated to you he could not talk to you because the caution was in the way."

Hamlyn replied, "That's right."

Mr. Byrne asked, "What was your reaction to that?"

Hamlyn hesitated and began searching through his notes again. "I am refreshing my memory," he explained to the court.

Mr. Gittens was on his feet again questioning the practice. He stated, "At this point I would indicate to the court that he has no recollection of his response to the situation posed by the Crown. He will however, check his notes to see what he had recorded as being his response at the time."

Judge Lang: "In the trials I have done, you usually hear the Constable say, 'may I refer to my notes?' In other words, there would be some indication he wanted to refresh his memories. But, I think Mr. Gittens is saying, is that when Sergeant Hamlyn is asked a question he goes through his notes to look for the answer."

Mr. Gittens: "Precisely my lord. There is no recollection."

Judge Lang: "What you are saying then is, we can only assume he is refreshing his memory. So you want to be sure he can't recollect."

Mr. Gittens: "My lord, my point is simply this. He has been asked a question that does not require the knowledge of a specific numerical number, time or place. It requires a recollection of his response to a certain event."

Judge Lang: "What was said of anything?"

Mr. Gittens: "Precisely, my lord. He has not given an answer to that question. What he has done instead is to go to his notes."

Judge Lang: "Right!"

Mr. Gittens: "In view of that I ask that it be put on the record that this witness is not recollecting by memory of what had occurred. He is in fact going to say what has been recorded. There is a distinction my lord."

Judge Lang: "On previous occasions all he says is that he has dates and times and numbers to jog his memory."

Mr. Gittens: "Right. The notes are to jog one's memory. If you have absolutely no memory at all of a particular event I believe that should be on the record, and then at the request of the court to read off what you recorded at that time. I would believe that would be appropriate rather than to give the impression you are jogging your memory when in fact you have no memory of the incident at all."

Judge: "I would think you would want the exact answer anyway, Mr. Gittens."

Mr. Gittens: "Yes, but it is essential to record what the sergeant is doing. He has no independent memory of what his reaction was. What he is depending on is what he has recorded at the time. That is the point that we wish to make at this stage."

At this point, the prosecutor entered the debate. Mr. Byrne observed, "It is an assumption he is making and I ask that it be made part of the record. Is this witness going to be refused the right at this time to access the notes that he took during the course of an investigation?"

Judge Lang: "Just a second Mr. Byrne. I think the question here is — if the sergeant can tell us whether he has to refresh his memory for the answer or not?"

Mr. Byrne: "Very well, my lord."

Judge Lang then put a question to the witness. "Do you have to refresh your memory for this answer?"

"Yes, my lord," answered Sergeant Hamlyn. "What was happening here was that Mr. Smith made the remark at one stage, that I had noted this morning, and I said to him after, let us forget the caution and I apologize. At that point I was checking to see if it was at this time. However, from the notes I made at the time I do not have that noted. So I have to say I do not know what my reply was to him at the time."

The defence argued strongly to prevent the police officer's statement from being admitted. Through questioning of Sergeant Hamlyn Gittens tried to show that the witness could not provide a detailed and accurate account of the controversial interview with Smith the morning after his arrest.

Mr. Gittens asked Sergeant Hamlyn, "Is it fair to say that whatever notes you have of that interview are not complete notes of that forty-minute interview?"

Sergeant Hamlyn replied, "That is true."

Mr. Gittens: "In other words the court will have to guess or depend on what you can recall of what transpired during the forty minutes for it to have a clear idea of what occurred?"

Sergeant Hamlyn: "Yes, my memory and Constable Baker's."

The defence wondered how the court could get a complete picture of the conversation that took place. Gittens suggested to the witness that, "the court will have to make it up to get a clear picture."

Sergeant Hamlyn answered, "No, not necessarily. I can talk about the conversation."

Mr. Gittens: "You can talk about the conversation as best you can recall."

Sergeant Hamlyn: "That is right."

Mr. Gittens: "What you do not recall the court will either have to do without or make it up."

Sergeant Hamlyn: "Or the court can get it from Mr. Smith or Mr. Baker."

The defence counsel then focused on the overall conversation held that morning between Hamlyn and Smith. Once more, Mr. Gittens attempted to show that the police account of the discussion was not complete. He asked, "You are telling the court that you have capsulized a two hour and eight minute conversation into two and a half pages, eight and a half by eleven of normal scrawl?"

Sergeant Hamlyn: "That is right."

Mr. Gittens: "Your notes if read out would reflect no more than ten minutes conversation."

Sergeant Hamlyn: "I would certainly agree."

The witness told the court he recorded in his notes each time Smith denied knowledge of the murder. This prompted Gittens to say, "You are limited by the fact that you made notes after the interview and you had to depend on your recollection of the conversation."

Sergeant Hamlyn replied, "That is right."

Mr. Gittens asked, "So there may be occasions where Smith in one form or another may have denied his involvement but which is not recorded?"

Sergeant Hamlyn: "That is possible."

The defence then argued the importance of complete notes in order to reflect the context of comments made by the accused. He suggested, "If there was some joviality going on and you were to say 'let us end this foolishness you know you are keeping me working overtime.' And there was a fair bit of laughter and if Smith was to respond to that and say, 'OK b'y. I'll plead guilty to it all right.' Unless you indicated in your notes that this was in a lighter moment, the mere recording of those words, 'Yes b'y I will plead guilty to it' would give a very different meaning to those words because of the context. Is that correct?"

Sergeant Hamlyn: "Yes, that is obviously correct."

Mr. Gittens: "Apart from the one lighter moment recorded in your notes, you do not have all the lighter moments that took place during those conversations. Do you have them recorded or not?"

Sergeant Hamlyn: "I have them recorded as I recalled them as I was making my notes. I recorded what I remembered of the content of the conversation." (Sergeant Hamlyn's practice was to record summary notes of the conversations with Smith immediately after the meetings.)

The Voir Dire heard evidence from Smith and several police officers regarding the questioning of Smith at Ferryland after his arrest. At the conclusion Judge Lang ruled that the statement made had been free and voluntary, and therefore was admissible.

An RCMP firearms expert testified that he believed that the gun taken from the harbour at Bay Bulls was the one which killed Jerome Fleming. Staff Sergeant Swim told the court that he had conducted tests on an expended shotgun shell found near Fleming's body. He said, "The tests found that an expended shotgun shell found near Fleming's body would have been fired from the shotgun found in the ocean near Smith's house."

The expert noted that Jerome Fleming had been shot at close range. To determine this he examined Fleming's clothing. He said, "The testing of three unburnt propellant powder grains contained on a swab of blood from Fleming's gunshot wound indicated a range less than four feet." At one point in the testimony Swim estimated the actual distance as two feet. The witness also told the court that the shotgun shells found in the ocean near Smith's house were similar to the shotgun shell found near Fleming's body.

When asked about the possibility of the gun accidently firing, the witness replied, "I do not think the gun would accidently discharge because of any mechanical problems. But the gun could accidently discharge without a trigger guard."

When cross examined by Gittens, the police expert conceded that the gun could have accidently discharged if Fleming was holding the gun towards himself and struck it against the arm of a car seat.

Margaret Maclachlan, an expert with the Serology section of the RCMP Crime Lab, gave evidence on blood, hair and fibre items relating to the investigation. The expert evidence showed that the shooting had taken place in the van. Maclachlan told the court that the blood samples from the van matched Fleming's blood samples. However, the expert found none of Fleming's blood on any of Smith's clothing. When asked to elaborate on this by John Byrne the witness explained, "It is very rare that I find blood from the victim on the accused's clothing in a shot gun shooting incident. I quite often find blood on the accused in cases involving a stabbing where the victim had bled a lot.

"If a body was bleeding badly, and someone picked him up and carried him, then, of course, you are going to find blood on him. That is if you are able to seize the clothes immediately. But, if, for instance, the clothes are put in a washer, blood will immediately dissolve in the water. There is absolutely no way I can test for blood or test for any blood factors in that particular case."

Maclachlan also gave evidence regarding samples of water and material taken from the Smith family washer about a week after the murder. In several public interviews Smith said that on the night of the murder when he went home for the night he tossed his jeans in the washer. However, the expert witness suggested that the washer had handled more than an ordinary wash load.

The witness told the court she had examined the samples in search of minute particles of human flesh. Police believed that the killer, in moving the body, would likely have picked up flesh particles. While the testing failed to identify any human flesh particles in the samples, Maclachlan testified that this did not eliminate the possibility that such evidence was contained in the samples. She explained, "The water from the washing machine was so dirty that any of the preliminary tests I used to check for the blood gave positive results. It was my assumption from this that it was due to the dirt and bacteria and other things that were contained in the water itself. The water was so dirty that I would not expect to find human flesh there anyway. Bacteria and other debris in it would interfere with any kind of testing that I would perform."

This prompted Gittens to interject, "The residue and sludge would likely be found in any wash day in a family with three children."

Maclachlan retorted, "I would not find that in my washer."

Other expert witnesses testified that the alcohol content in Fleming's blood was 110 to 120 mill at the time of death. The legal limit for driving is 80 mill to 100 mill. They found no hair or fibre evidence to connect Smith with the crime. This included carpet from Smith's house, the van and the area at the murder site.

However, the police experts had been ordered to search only for clusters of hair and not single strands. A cluster of hair would likely be found if the hair was grabbed in moving the body. Because the accused and victim knew each other and were together on the night of the murder, finding a single strand of hair would not have had any significance.

Paul Smith, brother of the accused, was subpoenaed by the prosecution to give evidence regarding the murder weapon. He told the court that Brian had owned a twelve-gauge shotgun, and that the barrel had been sawed off and the wooden stock sanded down. In response to Byrne's question, asking who changed the appearances of the gun, the witness replied, "I think the brother sanded down the barrel." Byrne interjected, "Was it the wooden part, the stock?"

Paul said, "The stock, yes. He sanded that down. I never paid much attention to it. It was just an ornament on the wall." Smith noted that the gun was originally owned by Jerome Fleming who sold it to Brian Smith. The witness was not sure when he had seen the gun at Brian Smith's house. He said it might have been two weeks before the murder or maybe two months before the tragedy.

However, when the prosecutor showed Paul Smith a

picture of the murder weapon and asked if that was the gun, Paul answered, "I would not be able to say if that is it or not. I would not know."

The prosecutor asked, "Taking a look at that gun and recalling the gun you saw mounted in your brother's home, is there anything major different about this gun from that one?"

Paul Smith answered, "I would not know. I never handled the gun. Jerome's gun or the one that was in my brother's home. I never handled it before."

Byrne asked, "But you saw it."

The witness answered, "Just glanced at something. It was like glancing at anything on the wall."

Byrne, "I take it then, you would not be surprised at all that this was the same gun."

Witness, "It very probably could be I would not know."

Byrne,"You just say, you just do not know positively if it is?"

Witness,"Yes that is right. I'm not quite sure if it is or is not. It looks like the same gun. Well all guns look the same, single barrel or whatever."

Rheal Luce from the crime laboratory's chemistry section testified that, "The metal filings found in Smith's house could have come from the shotgun found near Smith's house, or could have come from a common piece of pipe." Luce also told the court that the wood fibres found on a hacksaw which was taken from Smith's house were not consistent with wood contained in the gun stock.

Forensic experts also examined the green vehicle seat found at the murder scene. They found a Chrysler Corporation logo underneath the seat with the number 0172. This identified the year and date the car was made as January, 1972. Fleming's van was a 1972 Dodge two-tone, with red on top and black on bottom. A smear of black paint was also found underneath the seat.

The Crown called several witnesses who testified that they had seen Smith and Fleming together on the night of the murder. This evidence showed that Smith was the last person seen with Fleming before he was killed. Terry Williams testified that he saw the van go down the road at 10:30 p.m. toward the lighthouse. Mike Williams also saw the van around that time. He said he couldn't get through because the van was blocking the road. Mike Ryan, the undertaker at Bay Bulls, and Ted Williams were chatting near Ryan's home and recalled seeing the van drive by at 11:00 p.m. It was driving down the road from Smith's house and moving towards the Quay's Road. Fifteen minutes later it returned and went back towards Smith's house. However, they could not identify anyone in the van.

Forensic pathologist Dr. Eric Pike set the time of Fleming's death at about 11:00 p.m. on the night of April 5. Dr. Pike performed the autopsy on April 7, the day the body was found. He testified that Fleming died from shotgun pellets that entered the left side of his chest and went to the right side damaging many of his organs.

Dr. Pike agreed with RCMP experts that the victim had been shot at close range. However he said he could not offer any opinion as to the position of Fleming's body or the gun at the time of death.

The most damaging evidence against Smith came from the officer in charge of the murder investigation, Sergeant Douglas Hamlyn.

Hamlyn testified that during an early morning conversation on April 12, "Smith said, 'I did it, but I have to take my chances.' " The admission, according to the mountie's testimony came right after Smith indicated he expected problems in court. Hamlyn explained that Smith had said that he felt he did not have a chance in court and if he testified at the trial the prosecutor would tear him apart.

The witness told the court that Smith was talking as if he had committed the crime. He added that Smith suggested that he would prefer to serve his sentence at Kingston Penitentiary. During the conversation with the accused the sergeant had asked him how much time he expected to get. "Smith replied," Hamlyn said, "that he expected to get a five to ten year sentence because of the details of the death."

Hamlyn told the court that Smith also asked if the charge would be reduced from first degree murder if he pleaded guilty. The police witness testified that he explained to Smith that he could not comment on that. However, he did explain the court options which included: First degree murder, second degree murder, manslaughter, or acquittal.

The RCMP believed the motive for the murder was related to a drug deal. Sergeant Hamlyn affirmed that he told the accused that he believed the death was related to a drug deal. He suggested to Smith that the gun which killed Fleming was in a car the men had been in that night. Smith corrected him on that, testified Hamlyn, pointing out that the gun was in a van owned by Fleming. Smith added that he did not own a gun.

The chief investigator gave evidence on his confrontation with Smith at Her Majesty's Penitentiary on April 19. He revealed that he told Smith the gun and shells and other evidence had been uncovered by investigators in waters near Smith's house. Hamlyn related to Smith that he was confident the crime lab would confirm that the gun was the murder weapon. He had also disclosed to Smith that metal filings had been taken from his house. Hamlyn suggested that he was sure the crime lab would prove these filings were from the gun which had been sawed down and tossed into the ocean.

He told the court that during the conversation Smith admitted he did it. He testified, "Smith said as far as he was concerned all the evidence we had was circumstantial and there was nothing to say who pulled the trigger.

" 'How do you know Jerome was not reaching for the gun and pulling it towards him and the hammer hooked in something and set it off?' He said the hammer does not have to go all the ways back. It only has to go back so far to set it off.' "

Sergeant Hamlyn continued, "I told him it did not look

like that as far as we were concerned by the way that he tried to cover things up afterwards."

The witness testified that he suggested to the accused that the gun was brought into the van to use for armed robberies. He said, "Smith answered he was not into armed robberies. I told him we had reason to believe Jerome was. He said he didn't know anything about that."

According to Sergeant Hamlyn, Smith suggested that Jerome Fleming may have sawed the gun down. He told the court, "Smith said perhaps Jerome sawed the gun off in the house sometime when he was alone. Smith said, 'If Jerome yelled out and asked me for the hack saw, I would tell him it was on the bed or down in the basement. I would not ask him what he wanted it for. It could be to saw off a tail pipe or anything.'

"At that point he stood up and said 'The lawyer is ready to hang me for just being here with you; I cannot talk about it. I'm going for a long time. My wife knows nothing about it. I hope you will bring her in; that will keep her around and I will be able to see the family.' "

Smith had admitted to police that he was in the van with Fleming on the night of the killing. He told Hamlyn he last seen Fleming with the two men in the taxi.

Under cross-examination by Gittens, Sergeant Hamlyn noted that the most obvious and important contradiction in Smith's statements was his denial of involvement in the death of Fleming, but then saying several days later that he'd killed Fleming. Hamlyn told Gittens that because there were no other officers present when Smith gave these statements there is no one to corroborate or contradict them. Gittens asked the witness if and when he told other officers about the admission of guilt. The witness answered that he told other officers during a meeting of investigators on the morning of April 12.

One of the officers whom Hamlyn told was Corporal Hogg. He contradicted the claim made by Sergeant Hamlyn. Hogg told the court that Sergeant Hamlyn had informed him of the admission on April 10 or 11. Gittens reminded Hogg that Hamlyn had testified that the admissions were made on April 12. However, Hogg reiterated his claim that the information was given to him on the tenth or eleventh.

Before concluding his testimony, Hamlyn informed the court that a prisoner at Dorchester Prison offered to help the police in their investigation. Lawrence Maxwell Stanford had shared a cell with Smith during September, 1984. During that period, Smith often harassed Stanford. Among the crimes committed by Stanford were two incidents where he had struck his victims over the head with a hammer and a bottle. Whenever Stanford emerged from his cell, Smith would sing "Bang Bang Maxwell's Silver Hammer," a line from a popular Beatles' song. He sometimes asked Stanford if he thought he was Charlie Manson. When Smith did this, Stanford would return to his cell.

Another damaging piece of evidence showed that Smith had given away Fleming's van the morning after the murder, almost forty-eight hours before the body was found. Fred Power, a friend and neighbour of Smith's, gave evidence that Smith gave him Fleming's van on April 6.

Power's testimony indicated that he had visited Smith's house on the evening of April 5 to sort out a problem related to the registration of a car owned by Fleming. Fleming was present. The car had passed through several owners without the ownership being transferred. Although Fleming now owned it, the car was still registered in Smith's name. Smith had insisted that it be changed out of his name and Power was called to help. Fred Power bought and sold cars and was familiar with motor vehicle transfer policies.

Fred Power lived on the Alley Road, less than a half mile from Smith. In court, he described a deal he made with Smith for Fleming's van. He testified that Brian Smith called him the day before he learned of Fleming's death and asked to see him. According to Power they did not talk long on the phone. When he arrived at Smith's house it was 9:45 a.m. Brian offered him Fleming's van if he would take a motor out of a station wagon at a later time. Power agreed. Brian talked to Power from his front door. He said he had a cold.

Power told Smith he was rushed for time because he had an appointment at Manpower in St. John's at 10:00 a.m. Power testified, "Myself and Brian had a discussion about a station wagon up on back of his house. The motor and transmission were gone. He wanted me to give him a hand and take it out to replace it. He said he would make some kind of a deal in getting me a van that was outside his door. So we were talking mostly about the station wagon."

Byrne asked "Did you know who owned the van?"

Power: "Yes. But he said he would make some kind of arrangement with Jerome for getting the van."

Byrne: "He said he would make some kind of arrangement with Jerome. Where did this conversation take place?"

Power: "It was earlier in the evening or the evening before. We were down in the Smith residence between 6:00 and 7:00 p.m."

Byrne: "Was there any indication of this deal from Jerome?"

Power: "No."

Byrne: "Was this the first you heard of this deal, Friday morning?"

Power: "Yes."

Byrne: "Did you have any discussion when you were there Thursday evening. Did you have any discussion with Jerome about selling the van?"

Power: "No. Friday morning; and we left Smith's on Thursday at 6:30 p.m."

Byrne: "Were you expecting any call Friday from Brian Smith?"

Power: "No."

Byrne: "How long were you there that morning?"

Power: "About ten minutes."

Byrne: "How did Brian appear to you?"

Power: "Just the same. I didn't find any difference in him."

Byrne: "After this short conversation at the Smith residence what happened?"

Power: "I explained to Brian where I was going and I had to be in there by 10:00 a.m. I didn't have much time for talking to him. He mentioned the van. When I said I would see, he said go down and fire her and see if she will start. She would not start for me, so I left. I just got in my car and went on up and back to St. John's."

Byrne: "Why were you going to take the van at that time?"

Power: "We were discussing the van. He said he would give me the van if I would give him a hand to take out the motor in the station wagon. So I didn't have much time to discuss it. He said the keys were in the van if I wanted to take her."

Byrne: "How do you know the keys were in the van?"

Power: "I did not know if the keys were in the van. I just took a guess. If I was going along there and she would have started I would have taken her then. I went back to Brian's at 2:30 p.m. and he said the keys were in the van to take her up and see what you think of her."

Fred got the van started and took it to his driveway where he cleaned up the inside. He told the court he washed the motor cover, the dash, the windows outside and along the sides of the van. He then took his kids for a ride.

When the prosecutor asked Power why he had cleaned the van, the witness responded that it was a habit. He said, "Every vehicle I got yet I always clean the parts of it."

Under cross-examination by the defence, Power said it was not unusual for Smith to offer him a vehicle. He explained that in his circle of friends they swapped cars frequently.

Another witness who spent time with Smith and Fleming on the night of the murder was Randy Dalton. Dalton testified that he had no knowledge of the circumstances surrounding Fleming's death. He said he had been with the two on the afternoon and evening of April 5, but was not aware of any falling out between Smith and Fleming.

Dalton gave details surrounding an argument among them that evening over who would drive the van into town. Fleming owned a car and the van and intended taking both of them to the city. The van was in poor mechanical condition and all three wanted to drive it. Finally it was agreed that Dalton would take it and Jerome would follow him in the car.

Dalton said he left Bay Bulls at 7:00 p.m. and was supposed to meet Fleming in the city. When Fleming failed to show, Dalton circled back towards Bay Bulls. He went as far as the Goulds and returned to St. John's.

The witness testified that on the morning of Saturday, April 7, he telephoned Smith's house and was told Jerome had left there on the evening of April 5 in a Gulliver's Taxi. The witness said that Jerome had received fifteen hundred dollars from an insurance claim the day before he was killed. "He purchased the van for a couple of hundred dollars," said Dalton.

When cross-examined by Gittens, Power said he was then living in Oshawa, Ontario in a house occupied by Smith's wife and family and two other male boarders. He explained he was staying there until he could find accommodations. When asked if he had a relationship with Smith's wife, Dalton answered, "No."

Gittens then asked if the witness had a relationship with Mrs. Smith at the time of Fleming's death. Dalton answered, "I don't think that is any of your business." Judge Lang advised the witness to answer the question. Dalton replied that he did not have any relationship at the time. Neither was he aware of any difficulties between Smith and his wife or Smith and Fleming.

Early in the police investigation, Smith told investigators that there was friction between Peter Gulliver and Jerome Fleming. Hamlyn told the court that Smith said "Fleming was considering charging Gulliver with assault. He claimed that Ken Brown made the point that if Peter Gulliver goes to court he is going to jail."

Sergeant Hamlyn testified that Smith told him, "They got in a fight over Jerome using a cab unauthorized and this caused a problem. Gulliver didn't appreciate it and Jerome came out on the losing end of the fight."

The crown called Gulliver to give evidence regarding this dispute. Gulliver told the court he had last seen Fleming a month before his death. He testified, "Jerome was looking for his cab and pocket license which he had left in the car. We had a few words — a little argument — a little disagreement. We had a little fist fight. It started on Adelaide Street and it went up underneath City Hall where we finished our scravel.

"We argued over why he had been fired. He struck two cars up on Cabot Street. It was a night when we had freezing rain. He never notified me of the accident for two nights."

Gulliver testified that Fleming struck the first blow. He described the fight; "Jerome made a bang at me. I made a bang at him. Three or four punches were tossed both ways. He went up to the police and gave a report to Constable Howell." Gulliver also went to the police and gave a statement saying that Jerome made the first punch. No charges were ever laid in connection with the incident.

An inmate in a federal prison serving time for several violent crimes was called as a crown witness. He was Larry Maxwell Stanford, the same man Smith had harassed by calling him Charles Manson and "Bang Bang Maxwell's Silver Hammer." The witness claimed that while he shared a cell with Smith at Her Majesty's Penitentiary during September, 1984, Smith admitted killing Fleming. Sergeant Hamlyn told the court that

Stanford came forward, "because he felt what Smith did was wrong."

This prompted Gittens to ask Hamlyn, "If this man who wanted to help police because he felt what Smith did was wrong is the same man who was Canada's first hijacker; assaulted a woman in New Brunswick by hitting her over the head with a bottle and who tried to murder his sister?"

Sergeant Hamlyn: "It is the same man."

Stanford had been convicted in 1972 and sentenced to a twenty-year prison term for hijacking an Eastern Provincial Airways Jet from Labrador City to Montreal. The sexual assault and attempted murder of his sister occurred when he was on parole in July 1983. He pleaded guilty to the charge in October 1984 and was given a fifteen-year sentence.

The witness claimed that Smith had told him that he had killed Jerome Fleming with the same gun he had used in an armed robbery. Stanford surprised even the prosecution when he claimed that Smith was also involved in the murder of Dana Bradley. He said that at the time Smith told him this he was unaware of the Dana Bradley murder. Stanford explained that Smith did not actually name Bradley. He simply said he had participated in the murder of a girl on Shea Heights.

Stanford described Smith's attitude while at the penitentiary. He testified that Smith felt that although he committed these crimes, he would not be found guilty. The witness testified, "Smith said, 'I did it and there's no way anyone can prove it.' He said he used the same gun to kill Fleming as he used in an armed robbery. But he had cut it up to destroy the evidence." The conversation, according to the witness took place during September, 1984. The defence lawyer asked the witness why he did not tell police at that time?

Stanford answered, "Smith was already charged with murder and that was enough."

Robert Ryall, who was living with Fleming's wife Mary

at the time of the killing, was called to the stand. Police had learned that Ryall claimed he had killed Jerome Fleming. However, testimony showed it was not a serious confession. Ryall told the court that Jerome was living with him and Mary Fleming at the time of his death because he was out of work and had no place to stay. Jerome had a girlfriend at the time. Mary Fleming's daughter had told police that Ryall said he killed her father. However, Ryall told the court that was just a misunderstanding. He admitted saying it, but explained he really didn't mean it. He said the comment was made in the heat of an argument with Mary. She was upset over her husband's death and arguing with him. Ryall said the child overheard the comment.

The defence called witnesses to show there was no apparent animosity between Brian Smith and Jerome Fleming and that Fleming was receiving threatening phone calls. The defence also called as witness a cell-mate of Smith's to refute Stanford's testimony that Smith had confessed to the killing while in prison.

The victim's widow, Mary Fleming, testified for the defence. She told the court that Jerome and Brian Smith were, ". . . good friends." Mrs. Fleming said Jerome owned a gun at one point in their marriage but she did not know if he kept it. The witness said she had last seen Jerome alive on the morning of April 5 when he left her home to go to Brian Smith's at Bay Bulls.

Another defence witness was Fleming's girl friend, Cecilia Power, who testified that Fleming had received threatening phone calls which upset him. She testified that Jerome was concerned about the outcome of a fight he had with Peter Gulliver. She alleged that she had received two telephone calls from someone threatening Jerome and warning that he should drop assault charges against Gulliver, ". . . or he would be sorry."

The witness said Jerome received similar calls which always upset him for ten or fifteen minutes afterwards.

The defence called Patricia Smith, wife of the accused,

who told the court she had been pressured by the RCMP. She told the court that Sergeant Hamlyn told her Brian had confessed to the killing. She said he added that he felt she had helped Brian dispose of the body. Mrs. Smith was referring to the time she was questioned by Sergeant Hamlyn on April 9. The witness remarked that Hamlyn had told her both she and her husband could be charged and warned her that she could lose her children.

Mrs. Smith commented, "Hamlyn really scared me." She told the court that she told him at the time she did not believe her husband admitted to killing Jerome.

The witness recalled the night of April 5 when Jerome Fleming was killed. Brian arrived home between 11:00 and 11:30 p.m., she told the court. She added, he had been out in the van with Jerome and came into the house when two men arrived in a light-coloured car.

Mrs. Smith testified, "Brian went to the van about an hour later to get a soft drink and chocolate bar he had bought me. When he returned he said Fleming must have taken it when he went to St. John's." She told the court she thought she heard the van pull away at one point, but she was not sure if it was before or after her husband checked it. She concluded, "The van was still there the next morning."

To combat the testimony given by prison inmate Lawrence Maxwell Stanford, the defence called another inmate who at that time was serving a prison sentence at Dorchester Prison, New Brunswick.

Jim Newhook was in the same cell area at Her Majesty's Penitentiary with Stanford and Smith. Newhook had been sentenced to life in prison on April 1, 1984, for the murder of the night watchman at Bally Haly.

Newhook described Stanford's testimony as, ". . . completely untrue." He told the court, "Larry Stanford is a bit nuts and he had fixations about going to an institution in Quebec." The witness testified that he believed Stanford would do anything to go there and he testified for the Crown in order to get a favour.

Stanford had testified that Newhook was present when Smith admitted killing Fleming. Newhook described this testimony as, ". . . an out and out lie." He added that he never heard Smith admit to killing anyone.

Brian Smith took the stand to deny the charge that he murdered Fleming. He countered with a charge that Sergeant Hamlyn twisted the truth, fabricated evidence and omitted some evidence. The accused testified he did not admit to the murder to either Hamlyn or Stanford and he charged that two police officers threatened to beat him.

Smith explained he had agreed to talk with Sergeant Hamlyn after receiving the police caution because he was pressured to do so. He claimed Hamlyn had told him his wife might also be arrested.

Smith described the court trial as a, ". . . battle between me, Hamlyn and Stanford." He told the court that police witnesses had lied about conversations with him before and after his arrest. He charged that most of the evidence linking him to the death was fabricated.

Gittens asked the witness if he was aware of the seriousness of the charge against him. Smith answered, "I am well aware of it. It has been haunting me for a long time." When the defence lawyer asked the witness to describe his activities on the days preceding the murder he replied he did not remember specific events. He added, however, that he was helped in his recollections by the testimony given the previous day by his wife.

The accused told the court that Fleming and Dalton were helping him put a balcony on his house that week. He said he was paying them to go into the woods to cut and bring out sticks. He paid them at the rate of one dollar per stick. Smith explained, "I thought it better to pay them a dollar a stick to go in and get it, than go myself. I had so many other things to be at. Sometimes, I see up to twenty and thirty people a day."

The routine for Smith on the day of the murder was similar to other days that week. He said he sharpened all the axes and the chain saw, and they engaged in some friendly conversation before starting their day's work.

Smith testified, "It was about 3:00 p.m. when they came back from the woods. About ten people showed up at the same time. When Dennis Doyle showed up I jumped in his car and went off for awhile. It could have been an hour or so. Usually, he has a six pack or a dozen beer. When I left Dennis I came home and talked with friends."

The accused said they had another three dozen beers among them. He commented, "I do not drink very much, but on occasion when I do I probably have good reason."

According to Smith the discussion turned to Jerome Fleming's van. He told the court, "I was the one who told Jerome where the van was. It had passed hands from Pat Murphy to a fellow Crocker. I never had any interest in it. It's a pile of junk as far as I was concerned." He continued, "There would have been a discussion about selling the van. Those things are ongoing — I told him where to get it. We traded many cars back and forth for years. He realized the van was a piece of junk. Freddy Power is the fellow who would take something like that off your hands, and I know Freddy had an interest in it from Pat Murphy."

Later that night, according to the witness, Jerome expressed an interest in going for some beer. Smith testified, "The next day was Friday and I wanted to go to bed to get up early so I could get a few things on the go and get the weekend off — because we worked all week at the house — sometimes I put in sixty to seventy hours and the work is never done.

"Anyhow he wanted me to go to the club that night for a beer. I did not want to go. We did go to the Southern Discount Store a couple of times and I believe it could have been at 10:00 p.m. that night. I did see him lean over and talk to somebody in a car. I was higher up in the van. I was just sitting down in the seat enjoying myself, relaxed I guess. I did see him bend over and talk to a fellow in the car; it had a white roof. I never noticed who was in the car.

"I remember earlier that night. We pulled in by the

Southern Discount and I was on the passenger side and Jerome went into the store. There was a bunch of young fellas I knew from around the bay there hanging out. I did not see none of them called up here today in this trial."

Smith added, "I believe he could have discussed his disagreement with Peter Gulliver. He was kind of worried about it. There was no doubt about it. There's not too much more I can recall about that evening. Until about 11:00 when I noticed a car pulled up in front of the van just twenty feet ahead of us. He (Jerome) said there's a couple of boys from the stand and he still did not know what he was doing — if he was going to the club for a beer. I told him I was going in early regardless. Jerome was after working in the North West Taxi-Stand, Gullivers', Churchill Park Cabs. I even had my own taxi on the go for awhile and Jerome drove for me, so I do not know what stand he was talking about."

Brian Smith admitted to the court to being a drug dealer and he described his illegal activities. He said, "I sat at the door and when cars pulled up the boys handled it. If they were friends I did it. Less witnesses involved that way. I just had certain friends that I had dealings with and usually when they pulled in I let the boys take care of it. It is their department. I just go in and mind my own business. I believe it is no sense coming up here and denying it. There has been many allegations made. I have no drug convictions on my record."

Gittens interjected, "But you did deal in drugs?"

Smith answered, "Yes I did. I sold marijuana and hashish." He added that he expected to be arrested, ". . . sooner or later because Sergeant Hamlyn was on my case."

The accused went on to describe his reaction to the arrival of two strangers in a taxi. He said, "When the car pulled in at 11:00, I more or less got out of the van and walked up to the house. It was really dark there. It always is. No lights. Very narrow road. I walked backwards up the road to see if I could get an eye on who it was. I never got a response. I just turned when I got to my driveway and went on my way.

"When I came in she (wife) was in the washroom. The washer was in the doorway. She pulls it out there so it could reach the kitchen sink. I do not know if she was just finishing up there. She kind of said, 'Well that's it for the night'."

Smith testified that he also played backgammon and cards that night but could not remember much more about it. He remarked that soon after he went into the house he heard the van start up. He said, "Whether they pulled down the drive and took off out of there I don't know."

Gittens asked, "Did you check the van anytime that night?"

Smith answered, "I had no reason to, really. About an hour later I heard my dog barking, so I don't know what kind of activity was out by the door. Whether somebody was going up the road or whether the boys were back.

"I asked my wife if the dog was fed and she said, 'I do not think so.' I went out to get him food and that is when I noticed the van there. I had a big floodlight on the side of my house but it was out. So I went back in the house to get the flashlight. Then I remembered I had the flashlight down in Jerome's van that evening." When Smith went out he left the door open. He recalled it was a cold night and his wife shouted to him to close the door. She also asked him to get her a soft drink and bar.

He continued, "I went down to the van. I didn't notice anything different. I had no reason to. There was mention of a blanket. It must have been early that evening I carried down the blanket."

A key piece of Crown evidence was that Smith got rid of Fleming's van the morning after the killing. The Crown argued that Smith made a call to Freddy Power that morning to persuade him to take the van. Smith denied this allegation. He testified that he had another reason for calling Power. He explained, "I called Freddy Power —

not about the van — he was supposed to come to my house to get a quarter pound of weed. I fronted him with drugs and that is why he was calling down to my house."

Smith gave his version of how the van became part of the conversation. He said, "When Freddy Power came into my driveway he saw the van and asked, 'What is that — Jerome's van?' — and I said yes. Then I went into the conversation about the thing and Freddy was tickled pink, as you know he wanted the van before. He never had the money. He knew I wasn't in a rush for it."

The accused explained the deal he made with Power to give away Fleming's van. He said he told Freddy he had a station wagon which Jerome wanted to use as a taxi. The station wagon needed major repair work. Smith testified, "I bought it from Goose Bay, Labrador, and it was in good shape. Jerome wanted it. It had a sun roof and the back seat went down. It was a good wagon." He suggested to Freddy that he could take the van if he agreed to put the motor and transmission into the station wagon. Freddy agreed.

Smith continued, "Later that day Fred came back. I opened the door, I had the flu. We yelled back and forth. He said he was going to take the van then and it looked to me like Fred had clean clothes on. I saw him climb under the van. I said to my wife, 'Look at Freddy out there.' That's the way Freddy is. He would climb under a car with a Sunday suit on. Freddy got the van going and took it away."

Gittens asked, "What was the first day you became aware there was something going on over on the Quay Road?"

Smith: "Sometime on Saturday afternoon. We did not know exactly what was going on. We just heard there was a lot of mounties down there and there was a phone call from my mother. I'm not sure."

Gittens: "When was the first time you spoke to the police on the matter?"

Smith: "That night. Sergeant Hamlyn and Sergeant Avery."

Gittens: "Were you aware that Mr. Fleming was dead?"

Smith: "No. I knew there was a body down there. It had been found in the Keys (Quay's Rd.). But I did not know who it was."

The accused described the morning the police took him from his house to the Ferryland RCMP offices. He said when they came for him he called his lawyer. He explained, "I said there are police officers here at my house and they want to talk to me concerning the death of my friend. They told me I was not under arrest, but you have to go with us. He said, if you can help or assist them in finding out what happened to your friend go along with them. So that kind of settled me down a little."

The witness noted that he did not ask for a lawyer to be present at that time. He told the court he was treated all right and they were asking about his whereabouts that night. He said, "I was under the impression I was just there assisting them and helping them find out what happened to Jerome.

"They were trying to get me to recall the colours of the car. I know you just get a glimpse and you are gone and they were calling those things contradictions."

The continual interrogation caused Smith concern. When the police read the caution to him he asked for a lawyer and told them he did not want to talk anymore. He testified, "At one point they threatened to beat up on me. It was kind of a regular police thing, you know."

Gittens asked, "What was the nature of the threat?"

Smith replied, "Well they mentioned Ray Noftle. I know the guy — but had no dealings with him. They said you're not like Raymond Noftle — come on — you are a decent young fellow. You got a wife and kids — a lot of things on the go for yourself. We do not want to start beating up on you."

The accused explained why he agreed to talk with Hamlyn the next morning. His account contradicted the version presented by Sergeant Hamlyn. Smith claimed that while Hamlyn was asking about the gun he threatened to go to Smith's house and tear it apart until he found the murder weapon. The witness claimed that Sergeant Hamlyn warned, "I am going to pick your wife up if you don't start talking to me." Smith told the court that Hamlyn's threat to involve his wife and kids was the major factor in his decision to speak with Hamlyn.

Contrary to Hamlyn's claim that Smith was cooperative and anxious to talk with him alone, Smith insisted he was ready to explode. He testified, "I could have got very violent. I could have fought the man off. But I said no. Like I said, I was cautioned I was being charged. The way I look at it, the man would be down here saying I was violent, beating him up, fighting, resistance and everything else. So I just went along so long as there was no violence on me in that way. That was it. He never beat up on me."

Gittens focused on Hamlyn's evidence that Smith made several admissions of guilt to him. He asked Smith, "Sergeant Hamlyn has indicated that you made certain admissions to him. Can you indicate your recollection of what went on?"

Smith: "Well, there was a lot of things never said in this court room and a lot of things he took and twisted around completely. As far as admissions — I never made no admission to that man or any other man."

Gittens asked, "Sergeant Hamlyn said at one time you indicated the gun was not available?"

Smith replied, "Well, I would say there are a few things left out there. That is something he got twisted around you know to use against me. I got this figured out. On Tuesday morning he laid the charge. He never had no admissions. He never had nothing. On Wednesday, Baker went to Halifax with my boots and everything. He took them to the lab and they found there was no evidence and Thursday morning he had to make up something. You know it was too late then the damage was done. He cannot back out of it and he felt, more or less — to get me and they would find out who done it." Smith, however, did not explain what was left out or how Hamlyn had twisted the conversation.

He repeated his explanation for talking with Hamlyn saying, "The only reason I spoke with him was his threat to pick up my wife and children. I never said anything material to him."

Smith went on describing his irritation over his being questioned by Sergeant Hamlyn. He said, "He (Hamlyn) was steady bugging me, just bugging me. I mean he would come in and talk to me and I said 'Look I don't want you in this cell,' and he ordered a guard to open the door and came in anyway. What could I do? We did speak about the weather, the tea, the water and he adds an admission."

Smith offered an explanation as to how Sergeant Hamlyn came up with his claim that he (Smith) admitted killing Fleming. He testified that at one point he said to Hamlyn, "Listen, boy, if you fucking think that I am an ass, you fucking prove it. He took that, took out the ifs and fucking and made it an I did it."

Gittens jumped on this comment to illustrate to the court that Hamlyn did not write down everything of importance in his notes. He asked the witness, "You used foul language and none of that was indicated to the court. Hamlyn testified you never used foul language. Always a very good, proper person in your response to the sergeant?"

Smith answered, "Sure. He had to say that to put it across that way. I mean that is something else he has twisted around."

Smith talked about the discussion he held with Stanford. He told the court, "It was just a general conversation. Here we are just a bunch of men in the penitentiary. One man facing attempted murder; another convicted of murder. Any discussion that did go on centred around things happening at that time. The Bally Haly thing . . . it could have been a number of things. I never said nothing to Larry Stanford.

"First when I went into the unit I thought there was something wrong with Larry Stanford. I even mentioned it to Jim Newhook. I said, 'Listen Jim, what is it with this guy?' He told me Larry seemed to be all right. Outside of that I had nothing to do with him.

"Stanford used to get pissed off whenever we mentioned conversation about his sister. We used to say — Larry Maxwell Stanford, what are you like — Charles Manson. You used to like to listen to the Beatles singing *Bang, Bang Maxwell's Silver Hammer.* He used to just take off to his room."

It was during these early days of Smith's incarceration that he began focusing on the Donald Marshall case. He frequently talked about the Marshall case with other inmates, and in court drew a comparison between the Marshall case and his own. Smith recalled, "We talked about Junior (Donald) Marshall. That man served eleven years for a crime he did not commit and it pretty well was the same thing. It was a few police officers and some other guy from the penitentiary up against him. That is basically what put that man away." Smith described his own trial as, ". . . a battle between me, Hamlyn and Stanford."

Under questioning by his lawyer, Ernest Gittens, Smith charged that the evidence claiming he'd admitted guilt was fabricated. He insisted he had never admitted to the crime to either Hamlyn or Stanford. The accused added that neither did he suggest to Hamlyn that he preferred to serve his sentence at Kingston Penitentiary or that he felt he would get ten years because of the details of the death. The witness also denied telling Hamlyn he wanted to enter a plea to the charge the next day in St. John's Provincial Court.

Smith told the court he definitely did not tell Hamlyn he would like to get the matter over with to avoid dragging so many people into court. He charged that Sergeant

Hamlyn had fabricated the claim that Smith said he may as well do his time and be a free man in a few years.

Brian Smith did not stand up well to the cross-examination by prosecutor, John Byrne. Byrne questioned the witness about his claim he heard the van leaving the driveway when he left Jerome on the night of the killing.

Byrne: "Do you recall the question I put to your wife when she was on the stand about her statement to the police in this regard. She believed you both had heard the van starting up and I put it to her that she said in the police statement that she did not hear any van. As a matter of fact, the washer was on?"

Smith: "Yes, I can remember what she said in her testimony."

Byrne: "She indicated at that point in the trial, maybe she was confused when she was talking to the police."

Smith interjected, "Maybe she was, she had good reasons to be."

Byrne: "She indicated in her statement to police that the washer was on, and she indicated in her testimony to that, that may have been the case. She had a dark wash on and maybe had your jeans in there, as a matter of fact."

Smith: "That's also correct."

Byrne: "The question I am putting to you then . . . the washer may have distracted her hearing. Did it have any effect on your hearing?"

Smith: "No. There was no exhaust system on that van whatsoever. So we both would have heard that van."

Byrne: "Are you telling me that the engine when it runs had a very loud sound."

Smith: "Yes it did. Even idling."

Byrne: "If you never heard the van when it came back and if you were still up —"

Smith interrupted, "Well, it is a kind of a down-grade there and the vehicle would be in a drive position. The van wouldn't be so loud, because the idling is stepped down due to the fact the transmission cuts in."

Byrne questioned Smith about his conversation with

Freddy Power on the evening of the killing. He was particularly interested in determining if Freddy had agreed at that time to take Jerome's van.

Byrne asked, "Just after you indicated that you really did not know what your discussions were that night with Jerome, you went on to say that you said that Freddy had an interest in the van. Do you recall saying that?"

Smith answered,"Yes. I knew that Freddy would take the van.

Byrne: "Was Freddy mistaken when he said there was no discussion of the van?"

Smith: "He may — I do not say he was mistaken. I knew of that through Pat Murphy and just from my experience with Freddy that he probably wanted the van."

Byrne then focused on yet another inconsistency in Smith's story. Smith had testified that he and Jerome made a couple of trips to the supermarket the evening of Fleming's death.

Byrne stated, ". . . after his arrest all the police officers who questioned Smith in regard to him going to the supermarket — the story was the same. He was quite specific in that he remembered going to the Southern Discount only once that evening and that on the second occasion Jerome went and Smith did not go."

Smith replied, "That may very well be right to the best of my recollection. I had no reason at that time to remember the events of that evening in order like that."

Byrne challenged Smith's assertion that he had no reason to be as accurate as possible during the questioning. He commented, "You were being questioned in relation to the death of your friend. You are telling this court you did not have any reason to recall your activities."

Smith: "Those conversations that I believe were mentioned were on the seventh — the one when they were just asking me basic questions. I was not a suspect. On the tenth again; and again I was no suspect."

Byrne: "So really, you had no reason to. I put it to you, I think that when you say the tenth — you mean the ninth.

Smith: "The ninth, yes."

Byrne: "You were being questioned. You had talked to a lawyer. You had expressed enough concern to talk to a lawyer about it in advance. You were being questioned. You have at one point indicated that you felt you were a partial suspect that day?"

Smith: "I really do not know if I was a partial suspect or not. I just knew I was going to be questioned about it because of our closeness."

Byrne: "What I was putting to you, Mr. Smith — you were concerned about it and you are telling us now it was not a serious situation for you to try and recall your activities. To try and recall your activities accurately on the evening before when you were in the company of Jerome Fleming."

Smith: "Well, basically I guess I was trying to think of who he could have seen and all I saw was the top of a white car and I never seen him speak to anybody. I was more interested in something like that in recalling the drive up to the supermarket because we never spoke to nobody along the way at either time."

Byrne: "Then I ask you why you were so specific in your memory and recount to all those police officers of the fact that you went to the supermarket only once?"

Smith: "Well, I really cannot recall the events of that evening in that sequence or any sequence and I did not think it important at that time."

Smith denied saying he feared that if he took the stand the prosecutor would tear him apart. He claimed, "This is one area the RCMP twisted around." John Byrne noted that Smith's comments were inconsistent with Jim Newhook's testimony that Brian told him he did not think he could get a fair trial.

The prosecutor still had some questions for Smith regarding the van. He asked Smith, "Do you recall yesterday. You said Fred Power knew about the van. 'I believe I told Jerome about the van.' Do you recall that?"

Smith: "Yes."

Byrne: "Do you recall Fred Power saying he had not discussed that nor had shown any interest in the van to you or Jerome. Do you recall him saying on the stand his only contact with the van was with Pat Murphy?"

Smith: "Yes, but I recall saying somewhere along the line that Mr. Murphy was in my house previous to that and the guy that owned it before him, Mr. Crocker. I believe Freddy's name could have been mentioned there somewhere along the way."

Byrne: "Freddy said he did not express any interest in the van to you or Jerome?"

Smith: "No, maybe Pat Murphy indicated his interest in the van."

Byrne: "When you say Fred knew about the van, what you are saying is you got that from Pat Murphy?"

Smith: "Probably, I really cannot recall."

The prosecutor was persistent in his effort to show conflicting evidence between the accused and Fred Power regarding the van. Smith's giving away the van the morning after Jerome's death had become an important consideration in the trial.

Byrne continued his questioning. Referring to the evening of April 5th at Smith's house he asked, "You recall Fred saying the only thing you talked about was some marijuana and that it was not a good time to talk about it because there were other people there?"

Smith: "Yes, I can vaguely remember something about it. Like I said, I was pretty well speaking to everybody there but I believe Freddy's sole purpose of being there was to check on some marijuana."

Byrne: "Freddy would not be wrong then when he recalled to the court his testimony that he did not talk to you about any van or any deal. The only thing he talked to you about was the weed?"

Smith: "I do not know if that was to the best of his recollection or not. The van could have been mentioned. The van was there by the door."

Byrne: "You told the court you could not recall that one way or the other."

Smith: "No, I still cannot recall one way or the other but just the fact the van was there by the door. I would say that the van would have been mentioned if Freddy Power had interest in it before to somebody there or even myself. I can't recall that or even the discussion of the grass."

Byrne: "I put it to you that what you are saying is just supposition. You cannot recall, whereas Freddy Power specifically recalls."

Smith: "It is probably easy for Freddy to recall. Freddy do not do much. I was handling twenty different things there and Fred was just there for the sole purpose of whatever that was. But I would definitely say that if that van was by that door when Freddy Power was there, I am sure that they would have been mentioning it at that time. But at that time Jerome never had the van checked out so I mean probably she was not for sale there at that time."

Byrne: "In any case, you are not disputing what Freddy said in his testimony that there was no discussion of any deal concerning the transfer of that van on Thursday supper time when Freddy Power was there."

Smith: "I will not dispute that question."

Byrne: "Is Fred misleading this court when he says quite specifically the only discussion that morning (April 6, Friday) was of the transfer of the motors for the van?"

Smith: "Yes, it is perjury."

Byrne: "Do you recall telling Hamlyn and Avery that Power picked up the van unbeknownst to yourself?"

Smith: "I may have said it but I had no reason to think about it at the time."

During his testimony Smith testified that the gun parts recovered by the RCMP and presented as the murder weapon were similar to the gun he once owned but had given to Fleming. Paul Smith, brother of the accused, also testified that the weapon presented as evidence in court was similar to one he had seen at Brian's house.

The prosecutor questioned Smith about the gun and its disposal. Byrne asked Smith if he remembered telling Hamlyn about Jerome cutting a tail pipe or something.

Smith: "That piece of conversation may have come from someone else Sergeant Hamlyn had spoken to during the investigation. Because I have not looked at that gun yet. But if that is the gun, the top half of that barrel should have a saw cut into it which Jerome did saw that gun off."

Byrne: "Do you recall Jerome sawing the gun off?"

Smith: "Not that short, if that is the same gun."

Byrne: "I believe your brother recalled seeing the gun at your place and it was sawed off. You remember your brother Paul saying that?"

Smith: "Yes. I remember he was not sure if it was the same gun or not. He said it looked like that gun."

Byrne: "The gun in your home?"

Smith: "Yes, it was his memory."

Byrne: "Are there any other guns in your home that are sawed off?"

Smith: "No. The only guns I ever owned were two twelve-gauge guns. One, a pump action, I sold to Francis Coady."

Byrne: "So what you are saying on the stand now is that you know the gun was sawed off because before this Thursday . . ."

Smith interrupts, "Not sawed off that short. That gun was sawed off. If it is that gun, that would be another saw."

Byrne: "Do you know who sawed it off?"

Smith: "I believe Jerome may have himself. I am pretty sure it was sawed off."

Byrne: "Did he saw it off in your home?"

Smith: "No, the gun was sawed off long before I ever moved to Bay Bulls."

Byrne: "How did the barrel get out in the bay next to your house?"

Smith: "I do not know."

Byrne: "Hamlyn says that you, near the end of the conversation on the nineteenth of April, said that your lawyer was ready to hang you and you cannot talk to him anymore. You said you are going for a long time . . . my wife knows nothing about this."

Smith: "I cannot recall that."

When questioned by the police on April 7th, the accused had mentioned Gulliver's cabs. He also described the conflict between Peter Gulliver and Jerome Fleming. Byrne explored this part of the evidence.

Byrne asked, "Where did the discussion about Peter Gulliver take place?"

Smith: "Well, it would have to be in my van or in the house or maybe it wasn't even that evening. It could have been prior to that evening because you know, that thing was on the go a couple of weeks. I mean he was wearing the shiners for two weeks. So it could have been anytime. There was always a mention of Peter Gulliver."

Byrne: "So you are not really sure if you ever talked about Peter Gulliver that night, are you?"

Once again Smith was evasive. He answered, "I am not going to say yes for sure, but I am pretty sure there was a slight mention of it."

Byrne persisted, "You went on in your testimony yesterday that you discussed as I referred to you earlier, that you believed you spoke with Jerome Fleming about the disagreement with Peter Gulliver and then you said that a car pulled up in front of your van about twenty feet ahead. Jerome said there's a couple of boys from the stand. You indicated at that time, you knew that Jerome had worked at a number of taxi stands — you made no reference at that time to Gullivers. At one point in time you said 'I do not know what stand.' Yesterday in your testimony you indicated that what Jerome said was that there was a couple of boys from the stand."

Smith: "Yes, I remember that."

Byrne: "You did not mention anything about anybody

from Gulliver's or any Gulliver's taxi or anything of that nature?"

Smith: "Yesterday?"

Byrne: "Yes, you did not mention the name Gulliver's."

Smith: "Well, I said I was just trying to recall, you know I mean there was a lot. You just can't think of everything when you're up here in the box."

Byrne: "You indicated yesterday that what Jerome said was 'there is a couple of boys from the stand'?"

Smith: "Yes, I can recall something like that. I do not even know if Gulliver's was mentioned that night. I just probably put that there myself."

Byrne: "So what you are saying here to me now . . . you do not even know if Jerome mentioned Gulliver's that night at that time?"

Smith: "No, I really cannot recall that. He very well may have. I have said somewhere along the way that he did. I do not know."

Byrne: "I would put it to you, that you most definitely did mention Gulliver's almost immediately afterwards. You mentioned Gulliver's to your wife according to her testimony. When the police met you on the seventh, you very early in your conversation gave them that it was a Gulliver's cab, and you backtracked on your description and then volunteered information to the police about the dispute between Peter Gulliver and Jerome Fleming."

In his summation to the jury, Ernest Gittens argued that the prosecution's case narrowed down to one of credibility. Who would be the more credible witness: Sergeant Hamlyn or Brian Smith.

Gittens charged that Sergeant Hamlyn failed to give the court the true account of Smith's statements to him. The defence argued that the RCMP officer deliberately set up the investigation so credibility would be the issue. The defence attacked the quality of the police investigation. He told the jury there were aspects of the police investigation that caused great concern.

Gittens pointed out that Hamlyn put a great deal of

personal effort into the investigation. He added that Hamlyn quickly singled out Brian Smith as a suspect. Gittens suggested that Sergeant Hamlyn deliberately arranged one-on-one meetings with Smith so there would be no one to corroborate what transpired.

The defence lawyer argued that Hamlyn must have realized the case would come down to one of credibility. Hamlyn wanted credibility to be the issue, according to Gittens, so that he, an eighteen-year veteran of the RCMP would be believed.

Gittens implied that the situation set up by Hamlyn left Smith with no way to corroborate what he said transpired at the interview with Hamlyn, before and after his arrest. He went on to point out an inconsistency in Sergeant Hamlyn's account of Smith's alleged confession. He noted that while Hamlyn testified that the confession was given on April 12, Corporal Hogg had testified that Hamlyn told the investigation team of the confession on April 10 or 11. Hogg was certain of this.

The defence concluded with Gittens suggesting the Crown had not proven a crime had taken place. He told the jury, "No one knows exactly how Fleming died. There is not one iota of evidence of a planned and deliberate murder committed by Smith."

When John Byrne addressed the jury he dismissed Gittens suggestion that the Crown's case relied mainly on Hamlyn's evidence. He told the jury there was other evidence that must be taken into account.

The prosecutor scoffed at Gittens suggestion that no crime was committed. Byrne said, "If Fleming had killed himself, the van in which he was killed wouldn't have ended up at Smith's house, and the gun wouldn't have ended up in the ocean near Smith's house."

He said that Gittens was wrong to suggest the case is a contest between Smith and Hamlyn. He added that there was other Crown evidence. Byrne told the jury that crown witnesses had testified they had seen Smith and Fleming together on the evening of April 5 and the van was sighted on the Quay's Road where the body was dumped at 11:00 p.m.

The prosecutor described Sergeant Hamlyn as a very thorough investigator. He said, "It is not unusual for police to interview suspects in one-on-one situations." He added that Smith claimed evidence was fabricated or twisted around, but he never tried to explain how it was twisted. Byrne commented, "He was given the opportunity to refute what was said."

Byrne concluded his summation by expressing confidence in Hamlyn. He said Hamlyn had no reason to fabricate evidence against Smith. He described the sergeant as "a damn fine police officer who did not deserve attacks on his professional ability."

Justice Gerald Lang in his charge to the jury outlined the options facing them. He referred to the four choices: first degree murder, second degree murder, manslaughter and not guilty.

Judge Lang explained that for first degree murder, specific intent is required. The act must be planned and deliberate. He said, "The intent would be the person means to cause the death of another, or that a person meant to cause another bodily harm that would likely cause death.

"Second degree murder is not planned and deliberate but is the result of an unlawful act. Specific intent must be shown for second degree murder.

"Specific intent required for murder is not a requirement for a verdict of manslaughter. Manslaughter can occur when an accused is intoxicated by alcohol or is provoked."

Throughout his two hour charge, Justice Lang reviewed the evidence and possible verdicts. He explained that the fact several witnesses for the Crown and defence had criminal records didn't destroy or impact their credibility.

The judge also told the jury that the fact the accused had a criminal record must not be used to decide if the accused is guilty of a charge. He discussed the controversial evidence of Sergeant Hamlyn saying, "Just because I allowed the statements of Sergeant Hamlyn doesn't mean they were made or that they are the truth."

Contrary to the defence argument that the Crown had not proven Fleming's death was a criminal act, Justice Lang said he had no problem determining there was a murder.

At 12:30 p.m. on Thursday, February 20, 1985 the jury retired to consider a verdict. At 3:30 p.m. they asked for clarification of first degree murder, second degree murder and manslaughter. They also asked to review Hamlyn's testimony but then cancelled the request.

At 6:30 the jury was sequestered for the night because the heating system in the Court House broke down. Judge Lang quoted the criminal code which states a jury must be provided with adequate food, refreshment and lodging. He said their present situation was not conducive to the administration of justice. They met again early next morning and arrived at a verdict in about one hour. They had deliberated for a total of seven hours.

The jury found Smith not guilty of first degree murder but guilty of second degree murder. The judge asked the jury to retire again to consider a recommendation for a parole date. The jury made no recommendation. Neither did the Crown. The defence however, asked for the minimum period allowed by law.

Judge Lange sentenced Smith to life in prison with parole eligibility in ten years, the minimum allowed by law. The judge commented, "Enough grief had been caused the family." He said he was not going to make any speeches on increasing the minimum ten year sentence a person sentenced to life must serve before becoming eligible for parole. Two police officers escorted Brian Smith from the court room to begin serving his life sentence. Smith was placed under a forty-eight-hour suicide watch at Her Majesty's Penitentiary, which is the standard practice for any individual convicted of a major crime.

Meanwhile, Ernest Gittens was reviewing the trial, seeking out grounds for an appeal. An appeal to the Newfoundland Court of Appeal is not automatically granted. First, legal counsel must show to a judge of the appeal court that the appeal being made is not frivolous.

Less than a month after Smith's conviction, Gittens was arguing before an Appeal Court judge that his client had grounds to overturn his conviction of second degree murder and be given a new trial.

He based his argument on six points. First, he argued that, "The learned trial judge erred in allowing the respondent to at first limit the testimony of all the police witnesses to the investigation and then allowing the respondent to recall his police witnesses to give testimony dealing with the alleged statements of the accused forcing the appellant to split his cross-examination of police witnesses."

The second argument put forward by Gittens stated that, "The learned judge erred in ruling as admissible evidence for consideration by the jury oral statements allegedly made by the accused to Corporal Hogg and Constable Ryan of the RCMP."

Gittens' third point argued, "that the learned judge erred in ruling as admissible evidence for consideration by the jury, oral statements allegedly made by the accused to Sergeant Doug Hamlyn of the RCMP."

His fourth argument claimed, "that the learned trial judge erred in instructing the jury that as a presumption of law applicable to intent an accused is presumed to intend the natural consequences of his acts, without further instructing the jury that it is an inference which may be rebutted by evidence, and does not relieve the respondent from proving intent beyond a reasonable doubt. The instruction amounted to non-direction or mis-direction or a mis-direction as to purpose and effect of the alleged presumption."

Gittens fifth argument was that, ". . . the verdict is contrary to law."

The sixth argument concluded, ". . . and such other grounds as counsel may be permitted to address." Ernest Gittens asked that if a new trial was given, Mr. Smith wanted trial by judge and jury.

The Appeal Court judge listened attentively to the arguments put forward by Gittens on behalf of Brian Smith. He agreed that the arguments were not frivolous and the case was accepted to be reviewed by the Court of Appeal of Newfoundland. On October 24, 1985, the thirteen-volume manuscript of the Smith trial was in the hands of the Appeal Court. All that was needed to set a date for the appeal was for the defence and prosecution to submit their respective cases. Brian Smith was on the road to having three judges review his entire trial and rule on the issues which became so contentious in later years. However, the appeal was never heard. Why?

It appears that Smith was the architect of his own misfortune. Weeks after his lawyer succeeded in persuading the Appeal Court of the merits of Smith's appeal, Smith fired his lawyer. Records indicate Smith took this action due to, "a breakdown in client-solicitor relationship." For the seven-year period from 1985 to 1992 the Smith files gathered dust in the basement of the Court of Appeal on Duckworth Street. Not once during this entire period did Smith or anyone acting on his behalf contact the Court of Appeal to inquire about the status of the appeal or to seek direction. It seems incredible that Smith, who in 1990 began a publicity campaign to overturn his 1984 conviction, allowed his appeal to remain dormant for so many years. Especially, considering that the opportunity existed for him to have his conviction overturned and a new trial ordered. No one was stopping Smith from proceeding with his appeal.

Smith, however, argued that it was nearly impossible from inside a federal prison to take the necessary steps to have his appeal heard. He claimed the restrictions of incarceration effectively prevented him from pursuing justice. But in 1989 a significant development in the Newfoundland justice system inspired Smith to action and opened the door for his story to be told publicly.

Encouraged by the openness of the newly appointed Hughes Commission of Enquiry (into abuse at Mount Cashel Orphanage and the shortcomings in the Newfoundland justice system) and the vast nation-wide publicity it attracted, Smith seized the opportunity. He sent a plea for help to the Commission, claiming he was wrongly convicted of second degree murder and that his appeal had never been heard. The Commission assigned investigator Fred Horn to interview Smith at Joyceville Institute, Kingston, Ontario.

Horn was impressed by Smith's story and later expressed publicly the view that there was a fifty per cent chance Smith was innocent. However, after screening the information gathered by Horn, the Commission determined that the Smith case did not fall within its mandate. Consequently, Horn was not required to conduct an in depth investigation of Smith's claim. Smith was disappointed but not defeated.

Less than twelve months later Smith was given the opportunity to tell the public his side of the story of the murder of Jerome Fleming. The *Sunday Express* ran a three-part — although one sided — story on the Smith case.

The articles claimed that the trial came down to, ". . . the balancing of the credibility of two witnesses. Would a jury believe a respected police officer or a man who admitted in court that he sold drugs." It failed to point out that John Byrne had refuted that interpretation at trial and pointed out there was other evidence.

In the articles, Smith denied ever making the admission of guilt to Sergeant Hamlyn. He emphatically insisted his interviews with Hamlyn were not voluntary. Nothing new in the way of evidence was offered.

The articles simply echoed the defence position at the

trial in 1985. At that time the defence attempted to convince the jury there was no evidence of a crime and that police lied about conversations with Smith. Meanwhile, John Byrne methodically went through Hamlyn's evidence point by point with Smith, offering him a chance to explain how Hamlyn had twisted his (Smith's) statements. Smith's performance disappointed even his own lawyers. Smith himself sensed defeat when he suggested all the police officers lied in court and many of the jury members grinned in disbelief.

Smith's claim of innocence was given some credibility by comments in the article by Hughes' Commission Investigator, Fred Horn. Horn commented, "It could have been anybody. Anybody else could have done the thing. There was no direct evidence that he did it . . . no direct evidence to implicate him as actually doing the killing." Horn added that he was not saying Brian Smith was innocent and pointed out that the onus was on the crown to prove the case beyond reasonable doubt.

He explained, "I didn't think they proved it myself and I'm hesitant to believe that he did it. I feel there is a very good chance that he didn't do it. Because there's more to indicate to me that he didn't do it than he did."

At the trial, however, Byrne pointed out that there was evidence other than Sergeant Hamlyn's to consider.

Jerome Fleming was shot to death on Thursday evening, April 5. Brian Smith was the last person seen with Fleming before the killing. They were together in a Dodge van owned by Jerome Fleming.

Medical experts determined that Fleming was killed in that Dodge van. They also determined that death occurred around 11:00 p.m. At around that time witnesses saw the van moving from Smith's on the North Side of the Harbour towards the Quay's Road on the South Side. Fifteen minutes later the van returned heading towards Smith's. Forty-eight hours later the body of Jerome Fleming and evidence thrown from the van were found off the Quay's Road. Brian Smith was familiar with that area. He had been carting refuse to the area over previous days. The morning after Fleming was killed Brian Smith made a deal to give away Fleming's van.

The killer attempted to destroy two essential pieces of evidence. First he tried to conceal the fact the killing took place in the van. The second attempt to get rid of evidence involved the murder weapon. The killer was not content with just getting rid of the gun, but he also went to pains to disfigure it so that, if it was found, it would not be identifiable.

The small piece of body flesh and few blood stains left by the killer were detected by Sergeant Hamlyn and were enough to tie the van to the murder. Police divers recovered the murder weapon which had been filed down and cut into several pieces. It was located in waters near Smith's house. Evidence in court showed it was in Smith's house a week or so before the murder and Smith admitted to owning it at one time. Metal filings were found on samples of carpet taken from Smith's house. Experts' testimony was not conclusive on the metal filings but they claimed the filings could have come from the gun. Smith's comments to Sergeant Hamlyn and his inability to explain away the evidence against him gave the prosecution a powerful case.

The attempts to destroy evidence ruled out the possibility that someone was trying to frame Smith. When no other conclusion can be drawn from circumstantial evidence other than the crime was committed by the accused, such evidence can be used to convict. The circumstantial evidence combined with Hamlyn's evidence was compelling enough for a jury to convict.

Horn drew a comparison between the Smith case and the Donald Marshall case. He argued that the police prematurely arrested Smith. The veteran RCMP investigator claimed the police did not have grounds to arrest on first degree murder charges. He claimed that at the time the arrest was made there was, ". . . no conclusive motive, no murder weapon, no admission of guilt and no eye witness."

Horn continued, "It smacks very similar to the Donald Marshall thing really, in a way, because they got the accused and they built the case around him. They built the case around the accused and I mean they had no business arresting the person until they had grounds."

In the *Express* article Horn observed that if he had investigated the case, the selling of the van would leave him wondering about Brian's guilt. He explained, "I can't for the life of me see someone commit a violent crime such as that one and then bringing the evidence back to his doorstep. It just doesn't make sense."

However, considering the circumstances at the time, the alternate choice for Smith made less sense. To leave the van and walk back home would cause more complications than taking the van home after removing any evidence that a murder had been committed in it. An abandoned van would likely have led to the discovery of the body sooner than was the case. Also, earlier detection of the crime may have recovered some direct evidence like footprints, fingerprints or other evidence to help police build a case. The area was covered in snow that night. In addition, Smith would have had to get back to his house without being seen by any witnesses.

On the other hand it was less risky to be seen driving a van if the murder could not be connected with the van. If the murder had been committed on the Quay's Road there was also the problem of the murder weapon. Carrying it back through the community would be a sure give away. Tossing it in the woods or harbour, without destroying any distinguishing marks, would risk having the gun traced to its owner.

A more likely course of cover-up action would be to dump the body and destroy the evidence. The van did end up in front of Smith's home. Most evidence that a killing had taken place in it had been cleaned up. The killer took the time to file down the gun and cut up the gun stock.

Then he tossed the parts and the cartridges belonging to the gun into Bay Bulls harbour. He must have felt confident at the time that even if by chance all the parts were retrieved, it would not be identifiable.

With the van cleaned up, the weapon destroyed and no eye witnesses, the killer could feel confident. But police recovered the murder weapon and gave evidence that it had been in Smith's house a week or so before the murder and was at one time owned by Smith. The van had not been thoroughly cleaned and Sergeant Hamlyn detected a small piece of body tissue and some blood stains which enabled the police to determine the murder had been committed in the van.

The *Express* article suggested that the evidence of two eye witnesses that the van was seen coming from Smith's house and going in the direction of the Quay's Road was weak. This was an important part of the Crown's case because the sighting took place at 11:00 p.m. and medical opinion determined that Fleming had died about 11:00 p.m. The article quoted John Byrne as telling the jury, "They [Mike Ryan and Ted Williams] saw this van drive from one end of the bay right around and out the Quay's Road on the other side." The writer then noted, "The only problem was that the two witnesses could not see any part of Quay's Road from where they were sitting." The van could have been heading anywhere including out the main road to Witless Bay. The Quay's Road was only one of a number of possibilities."

However, the witnesses' testimony was that the van was moving towards the Quay's Road. They did not say they saw it on the Quay's Road. But the body was dumped on the Quay's Road. Since the van's trip from Smith's house to wherever it went and back was about fifteen minutes, and considering Fleming was killed in the van and the body dumped at the Quay's Road, where else could it have gone?

The only conclusion to be drawn from the evidence

was that the van did go to the Quay's Road at around 11:00 p.m.

Justice David Watt, of the Ontario Supreme Court in his book, "Appellate Jurisdiction," explained, ". . . an appeal against conviction can be allowed if there has been a substantial legal error at the trial. Legal error will only avail an appellant where a substantial wrong or miscarriage of justice has been thereby occasioned.

"An appeal from conviction is also allowed where the court is of the opinion that upon any ground there was a miscarriage of justice."

The strength of Brian Smith's effort to get a new trial was not in the lack of evidence against him but in the legal arguments developed by the man Smith fired in 1985, Ernest Gittens. Gittens argued that the evidence submitted by the Crown did not support a conviction of second degree murder. But he also claimed that errors in law were made in terms of admissibility of statements alleged to have been made by him.

The defence lawyer also suggested that Brian's constitutional rights were violated during his period of confinement at Ferryland. Gittens argued, "In a technical sense he was given the opportunity to contact counsel. So the legal basis was met. As to whether or not they should have gone ahead to keep on interviewing him for that week, I've got a bit more problem with that. If a person says I do not wish to be interviewed, I do not want to give an answer, your continuous interrogation of that person constitutes a breach of that person's Charter of Rights."

Gittens continued, "The jury was being asked to assume that all the evidence pointed to Brian Smith as the killer and then to make the next inference that he intended to do it. It seemed to me two logical links they had to make and they made it against him. I suspect it's because he did not come across as a very believable individual on the witness stand. As far as whether they legally proved it or not, I have a problem with that."

In the *Express* article Smith discussed his firing of his

defence lawyer. He explained, "There were a lot of questions at the trial that should have been asked all of the witnesses, that were not asked. And I let it go at the time. Basically, I wanted a lawyer who was ready to expose some of these people publicly that were involved in my case." He stressed he would not be satisfied with a court-appointed lawyer. Smith said he wanted a lawyer who would reopen the case and let Brian Smith have his say.

He discussed the problem of getting a lawyer from within prison. He said, "For me to get in contact with anybody whatsoever, it would take three weeks to get hold of my classification officer and finally make a phone call. For me to make phone calls right here, I got to phone lawyers I don't even know and ask them to accept charges." He noted that his ex-wife and his brother Paul tried in Newfoundland and Ontario to get him a lawyer but they had no success.

Brian told the media in 1990 that he often told prison staff he was innocent. He commented, "They answered, 'Well, I guess only you and God knows' and I would say, 'Yeah and whoever done it.' "

Gittens told the *Express* that at various points throughout Brian's incarceration, pressure was applied to discontinue his appeal and admit guilt. Smith cited as an example an incident when he requested a transfer to work camp. He claimed he was turned down because he insisted he wanted his appeal heard.

Smith told the *Express*, "I want a fair shot at an appeal with a lawyer I can trust and I want to be there for every word that is said, so that I know what is being said and what the arguments are."

By 1992 the Smith transcripts were still gathering dust in the basement of the Appeal Court. Seven years had then passed and nobody had bothered to contact the Appeal Court to expedite the matter. On June 10, 1992, the Court of Appeal sent a letter to the Newfoundland Legal Aid Commission regarding the neglected appeal.

Pauline Butler wrote, "The Chief Justice has directed me to write you about this above matter. There has been no activity in this matter since the transcript of evidence was filed on October 24, 1985.

"If it is not your intention to proceed with the appeal would you be good enough to file a notice of discontinuation pursuant to rule 57-17.

"If no further step is taken in this matter I am directed to pursue rule 57-18 to fix a time for the court to consider whether to dismiss the appeal."

The senior staff solicitor for the Newfoundland Legal Aid Commission, Dennis McKay, replied to the request. He stated, "Please be advised we have passed your letter on to David Eaton who we understand presently represents Smith. We further advise Mr. Ernest Gittens is no longer associated with the Newfoundland Legal Aid Commission."

Mr. Eaton promptly responded to the inquiry from the Court of Appeal. He advised that he was in the process of preparing a factum, ". . . therefore request no action be taken by the Court concerning the dismissal of this appeal." However, Smith was not happy with the efforts of his lawyer and decided to replace him. Smith turned to well known Newfoundland Criminal Law attorney, Jerome Kennedy.

Meanwhile, during April 1993 while at Joyceville Institute in Ontario, Smith learned he had advanced cancer of the lung. Time was running out for Smith. His lawyer succeeded in having him transferred from the federal prison to St. Clare's Hospital at St. John's while waiting for his appeal to be heard. Soon after arriving he was moved to the Health Science Centre and placed under the care of Dr. Kim Hong, radiologist and oncologist with the Newfoundland Cancer Treatment Research Foundation.

A combination of chemotherapy and antibiotic treatments improved Smith's condition. Dr. Hong noted, ". . . the infection cleared and cancer improved. He is well enough to be discharged and continue as an outpatient."

Because of the need for continued monitoring and treatment, Dr. Hong recommended that Smith be kept in the city area. He gave a letter to this effect to Jerome Kennedy and Kennedy used it in Court to request Smith's release so he could stay with his family. Considering the seriousness of Smith's medical condition and recognizing the time needed to get the appeal heard, the court granted Kennedy's request. After a lengthy battle Smith was finally free.

Smith gave a sworn statement to the court. He stated:

1. I have maintained since the date of my conviction for the murder of Jerome Fleming on February 22, 1985, that I was wrongfully convicted and that I am innocent of this crime.

2. A breakdown in the solicitor-client relationship between Mr. Gittens and myself, another lawyer was not retained until I retained the services of David Eaton, October 1990.

3. I never gave up hope of having my appeal heard.

4. I was without service of legal counsel from March, 1985 to October, 1990.

5. I took whatever avenues open to me to demonstrate my innocence. In July, 1990 I approached the Hughes Commission — as a result I got a visit by Fred Horn, investigator for the commission.

6. I approached various news outlets from September, 1990. A three-part series was published in the *Sunday Express* on my case.

7. I contacted CBC in St. John's and a documentary was broadcast.

8. I also took other steps to retain counsel but was unsuccessful in that respect.

9. I retained the services of David Eaton. Between October, 1990 and April, 1993 Mr. Eaton did not appear to take any steps to pursue my appeal, so in April, 1993 I contacted my present lawyer Jerome Kennedy.

10. Although discussions with Correction Services Canada and Parole Authorities about allowing me to live

at the Hostel at the Health Science, I have no reason to believe I will receive day parole or full parole when I become eligible. Also, because I maintain my innocence it adversely affects my relationship with these various authorities.

Smith's dying wishes were that he be cleared of the 1984 conviction. He stated, "Two main wishes before I die: that I have my appeal heard and, hopefully, to have my innocence demonstrated; and to return to live with my family in Bay Bulls. Having been deprived of the opportunity to watch them grow up I would now like to regain again a little of my dignity before I die."

On February 3, 1994 Brian Smith passed away. His appeal will never be heard.

Smith's conviction and subsequent appeal attracted little attention and no controversy in 1985. No one but Smith and perhaps a few close friends and relatives felt he was innocent. When he passed away in 1994 his three-year public campaign for an appeal and a new trial left an impression in the public mind that Brian Smith had gotten a raw deal from the Newfoundland justice system. Did he, really? You be the judge.

THE SAND PITS MYSTERY

A BIZARRE EPISODE IN Newfoundland criminal history took place during the summer of 1957. Its surprise ending also marked the beginning of a mystery that has remained unsolved for almost forty years. Many around St. John's remember it as the perfect crime.

The incident was first brought to light by three young boys who made an accidental and gruesome discovery at the Sand Pits. This area was located off Elizabeth Avenue, which was outside the St. John's city limits at the time. Thirteen-year-old Oswald Oliver, his younger brother Howard and a friend Albert Benson, had chosen to spend July 28, a warm, dry summers day, fishing at the Sand Pits. When the boys had tired of fishing, they turned their attention to the excitement of building a camp fire.

The boys began combing the area in search of dry wood. Benson was first to catch a glimpse of a bundle with what seemed to be a human arm protruding from it and covered with blood. Oswald Oliver was close behind and was not startled by the discovery. He recalled, "I thought at first it was a dog and I kicked it. Then I saw it was a baby and it was burned."

Oliver picked up a brin bag and placed it over the head of the charred corpse. The trio then ran all-out to their homes on Empire Avenue where they excitedly told of their grizzly discovery.

Sergeant Ron Evans of the Newfoundland Constabulary responded to the call from the boys' home and escorted them back to the scene of the find. He described the location of the bundle and body as, ". . . about eight feet off the road to the west of Elizabeth Avenue." It was burned considerably and covered with charred papers, tissue and bits of clothing. A bundle of clothing was found nearby.

The police gathered the body and the bundle of clothing and went first to Constabulary headquarters at Fort Townshend, then to RCMP headquarters at Kenna's Hill. The case was turned over to the RCMP because the area where the body was found was outside city limits at that time, and therefore within RCMP jurisdiction.

From the RCMP offices the body and bundle were taken to the morgue at the old General Hospital. While at the morgue another surprise was revealed to investigators, which complicated their investigation. One RCMP officer at the morgue was Corporal Patrick Noonan. While the pathologist examined the dead infant, Noonan opened the bundle of clothes retrieved at the Sand Pits, and discovered the body of a second infant. According to Noonan, ". . . the body was in a decomposed state and dead for some time. It appeared to have been tidily and properly dressed. It was in a mummified condition, flattened to a thickness of about three inches and dried and hard like a piece of board."

The first baby discovered was wrapped in a blue blanket. Part of the sleeve of a rose coloured sweater and a small piece of white cotton sheet remained unburned and partially covering the child. The second child was dressed in a baby's night dress with handiwork around the neck. Two other night dresses were found in the bundle.

Who were the children? Were they alive before being burned? Who did it? Were there any witnesses? Why? These were some questions confronting the RCMP as they took charge of the investigation that night.

The next morning while police pondered the mysterious baby deaths, newspaper headlines and radio broadcasts told the tragic story of the Sand Pits babies to a public unaccustomed to this type of brutality.

Taxi driver Eli Dooley,* was having breakfast with his wife just as *The Daily News* arrived at his home. Dooley was already puzzling over what to do about a strange set of circumstances he had encountered several nights before.

At 10:30 p.m. on Tuesday, July 25, Eli was called to pick up a fare at Theatre Pharmacy on Queen's Road. Dooley recalled, ". . . the caller had a foreign accent and I couldn't understand it very well." When he arrived at Queen's Road a man and woman came out and got into the back seat of his car. The man instructed him to drive around the city, which he did for forty-five minutes. He then dropped the man off at the Army Dock Gates at the waterfront.

When the man left the car, the woman asked Dooley to do a job for her. He agreed. He drove the lady to her apartment at 92 Queen's Road. She went inside and returned minutes later carrying a carton and a newspaper that she placed on the back seat. The lady then directed Dooley to drive her to the Sand Pits. She appeared to be familiar with the area and she selected a certain spot to stop.

Dooley didn't ask any questions. The woman got out of the car, took the carton and papers and walked back the road a few feet. Dooley turned the car around in time to see her strike a match and set fire to the paper that she had wrapped around the box. They remained at the site until the fire went out, then he dropped her off on Duckworth Street. It was after 1:00 a.m.

The episode aroused Dooley's curiosity, and on Thursday night he decided to return to the site and

---

* Eli Dooley is a pseudonym

attempt to detect what the woman had burned in the box. By then, however, the area had been cleared up by police who had been there that afternoon. Dooley, left the area even more baffled.

Now, reading the *Daily News* over his morning coffee, Eli Dooley understood what had actually happened that Tuesday night and why the area was now cleared of evidence. He related the entire story to his wife who agreed that he should go to the police.

After Dooley related his experience to Constable Coady, he was asked if he could identify the woman. He replied, "I know her to see her and I know where she lives. She's a mainlander and she lives in a flat at 92 Queen's Road."

"Are you sure you can identify her?" asked Coady.

"Well, she's been in my car nine or ten times over the past couple of years. I'll have no problem identifying her," replied Dooley.

This information gave the police their first break in the case. They now had a suspect. At 2:00 p.m. Constable Coady and Corporal Noonan arrived at the 92 Queen's Road apartment. They were greeted at the door by Linda Doane.* The thirty-seven-year-old woman had moved to St. John's from Halifax several years before, after the break up of her marriage.

Constable Coady told her he had information that she had been seen bringing a carton out of her house to a taxi earlier that week. Linda denied the claim. Coady presented a search warrant and the police thoroughly searched her apartment.

Corporal Noonan removed ashes from the fireplace and gathered some papers and some cotton fabric. These items were taken to police headquarters for examination. Constable Coady then accompanied Dooley to the Sand Pits. The witness picked the exact spot where police had

---

* Linda Doane is a pseudonym

found the dead babies. Coady was convinced that Dooley had witnessed the crime. He arranged to have Linda Doane brought to police headquarters to participate in a lineup with five other women.

Dooley had no problem identifying Linda as the woman he had driven to the Sand Pits on the night of July 25. He pointed her out on three separate occasions from three different positions in the lineup. The suspect now became the accused. The police obtained a signed statement from Doane and then placed her under arrest. She admitted knowing Dooley in a casual way but denied any connection with the incident.

Linda Doane was, ". . . charged with dumping the body of a child by attempting to burn it." Police had learned that Doane had been born at Enfold, Saskatchewan in 1919. She had been christened Michelle Semenchuk but changed her first name to Linda before marrying a Newfoundlander in 1953.

Linda Doane hired St. John's lawyer, Sam Hawkins to defend her against the charges. After hearing Doane's story, Hawkins expressed some doubts about the legality of the charge brought against his client. He explained to her that the charge under the Criminal Code related to a mother disposing of her child's body. She had claimed that the babies were not hers and that she had not been pregnant since 1953.

Several days after the meeting with Hawkins, Linda Doane walked into the offices of Dr. John B. Ross, requesting an examination to determine if she had given birth recently. When the Doctor completed the examination, she told him of the charges pending against her. The result of the medical examination was given to Hawkins and included as part of his defence strategy. Dr. Ross had verified that the babies could not have been Linda Doane's because she had not recently given birth.

The police quickly completed their investigation and the case went to court mid-August 1957, less than two months after the crime. The case was tried by Magistrate

Hugh O'Neill. An experienced crown prosecutor, Harry Carter, represented the Crown. Carter had been involved in the prosecution of many high profile trials during the 1950s and was well known to the public. When the trial got underway the court room at the old Court House on Duckworth Street was filled.

The key witnesses for the prosecution were: Eli Dooley, pathologist Dr. Joseph Josephson and several RCMP officers including Corporal Pat Noonan, Constable Hugh Coady and Constable John Mullaly. Coady testified that he had taken a statement from the accused shortly before her arrest on June 28. This statement became a controversial part of the trial.

Coady read the entire statement to the court. In it Doane denied any knowledge of the incident at the Sand Pits. She said she had not been pregnant since 1953. When police questioned her about the blood spots found on her bed she told them, ". . . the spots were there from my pregnancy in Halifax in 1953." Doane had admitted in the statement to knowing Dooley but denied going to the Sand Pits with him at any time. She knew him only by sight as a taxi driver with whom she had driven on many occasions.

Linda Doane recalled for police her activities on the night of the offence. She told police she had gone for a stroll and returned home by midnight. The witness again denied being in Dooley's taxi or going to the Sand Pits.

The accused noted that her landlady had come up to her apartment during the night and asked if she smelled gas. Doane's apartment was on the third floor.

During cross-examination of Coady, Hawkins raised the ire of Carter by asking, ". . . if any money had been paid to the witness (Dooley)?"

"No!" replied Constable Coady. Carter objected to the question but Magistrate O'Neill ruled that there is nothing to prevent that type of questioning. He added, ". . . but it could have far reaching implications."

The defence questioned the methods used by police to set up the identification lineup. Hawkins attempted to have evidence resulting from the lineup barred. However, he was unsuccessful. He told the court he was not satisfied with the manner in which the identification took place. He suggested the information which led to the arrest was incomplete.

Hawkins noted that Doane was conspicuous in the line-up because she was the only one wearing a bandanna. Coady explained, "She was wearing one when picked up, but I can't recall if she wore it in the lineup." When Hawkins questioned Coady on the type of women selected for the lineup, Harry Carter objected.

Hawkins asked, "What description did you have of the woman Dooley took to the Sand Pits on the night in question?"

Coady answered, "I was told that she was a mainlander living at 92 Queen's Road."

"And that was the only description of the woman you had!" declared Hawkins.

The second witness, Constable J. Mullaly, told the court that Doane had $1400 on her when she was picked up by police on June 28. He testified that she had two handbags containing $1415.96. This time it was Hawkins who was on his feet objecting. He argued that ". . . it is irrelevant and could prejudice issues for the defence." O'Neill agreed.

Next for the prosecution was the provincial pathologist, Dr. Joseph Josephson. Spectators gasped as the doctor raised the possibility the babies had been murdered. He told the court that both infants had been full term and were alive when born. To clarify his evidence Josephson classified the bodies as baby A and baby B.

Baby B was the larger baby and the first one discovered at the Sand Pits. Baby B was eight pounds and measured fourteen inches in length. The charges against Linda Doane were related to baby B.

Dr. Josephson testified, ". . . the areas most badly burnt, were the face and sides of the head, the forearms, feet and abdomen. There was air in the lungs and bowels indicating the child was alive when born.

"Skull bone structure indicated the child was not alive more than three days," Dr. Josephson said. He concluded that there was no evidence of smoke in the lungs. The baby was dead before it was burned. The witness could not be specific on how long the babies had been dead and he suggested, ". . . no more than one to three weeks. The babies did not die where they were found because there was no evidence of parasites on the body, or that they had been attacked by rats or mice."

Dr. Josephson continued, "A hole in the outer abdomen of child A could have been caused by burning." The pathologist could not obtain any specimen of blood on which to base any conclusion or relationship. He was not sure that blood grouping could establish a relationship excepting in cases of identical twins. Dr. Josephson testified baby A was dead longer than Baby B. He noted that the bodies were not at the site very long, ". . . because the condition of the clothing did not suggest exposure for long to the elements."

Due to the poor condition of the bodies Dr. Josephson could not determine any relationship between the two.

Dr. Josephson told the court that while he couldn't find the exact cause of death, ". . . it could have been caused by smothering." On cross-examination he testified that he could not rule out the possibility of death from natural causes.

The post mortem showed that the babies were recently born, and generally scorched and burned. Baby B was wrapped in partly burned and scorched materials. It was covered in a nightgown of good quality. The pathologist told the court that ". . . the face, hands, abdomen, legs and arms of the body were scorched. The back was least burnt. B was much better preserved than A." The autopsy found no evidence of violence. However, Dr. Josephson said the babies likely died at separate times. He explained to the court that the rate of decomposition depended on the temperature and other environmental conditions.

The Crown depended on the strength of Eli Dooley's testimony in its attempt to convince the court of Linda Doane's guilt. The police accepted Dooley as a credible witness because he had led them to the site where the bodies had been found. Dooley had also identified the accused in a police lineup. In court, he told his story again and when asked if the woman he drove to the Sand Pits was in the court room, answered "yes."

Carter asked, "Will you point her out for the court?"

Dooley looked directly at Linda Doane and answered, "It was her!"

Carter asked, "Are you sure?"

"Yes. I am sure. If you drive a party eight or ten times you know the party."

The witness explained he first drove the accused three years before when he picked her up at the Balsam Hotel.

Eli Dooley remained unshaken in his testimony under cross-examination. He held no doubts that Linda Doane was the woman he had driven to the Sand Pits that night.

Sam Hawkins grilled the witness further. "Were you suspicious of wrongdoing?"

The witness replied, "No. I thought it was unusual, but I saw nothing strange in it."

Hawkins continued his questioning, "Why didn't you look into the carton?"

Dooley answered, "I did not want to become an accessory. I believe in minding my own business."

"Why didn't you get out of the car at the Sand Pits?" queried Hawkins.

"I've been driving a cab for a long time. I learned long ago to mind my own business. I felt if Miss Doane had clothes to burn it was her job," answered Dooley.

"And you were not at all suspicious," quipped Hawkins.

"No," replied the witness. "I told my wife and she was suspicious."

Hawkins looked into the eyes of Eli Dooley and observed, "I suggest you knew what was in the parcel." Dooley answered with determination, "No, I did not."

The defence asked the witness if the accused had explained why she was burning the material. Dooley replied that, "She stood by the car while the fire burned and explained it was just dirty underclothing. She said she did not want them to fall into anybody's hands and she wanted to dispose of them herself."

According to Dooley, Doane told him that someone had stolen her garbage pail. She felt that if she put the clothes on the street they would be torn apart. The witness claimed Doane had told him the box contained a slip, a girdle and panties. Because they were blood stained, she wanted to dispose of them herself.

The next day the *Daily News* head line read, "Fingered by Cab Driver — Body Burning Trial Starts." The trial attracted intense public interest. People speculated that the babies had been killed to cover up the involvement with prostitutes of some prominent names. However, no evidence surfaced at the trial to support that belief.

A key witness for the defence was Dr. John Ross. He testified that he examined Linda Doane on July 3 and certified she had not delivered a child in the previous four weeks. Dr. Ross based his findings on x-rays taken and Doane's medical history. He said she told him she married in 1952, delivered a stillborn child in 1953 and separated in 1954.

The defence witness noted that there was evidence of a previous birth but not over recent weeks. Following the testimony of Dr. Ross the court adjourned until the next day.

When the trial resumed, the defence introduced sensational evidence. Hawkins called to the stand a witness who gave Linda Doane an alibi for the time of the crime. The move upset the police and prosecutor because the existence of such a witness had not been made known earlier.

John Maloney was a partner with Avalon Paint Co. The company had headquarters in St. John's and carried on work all over the island.

Maloney was at Argentia when Doane was arrested and he had not seen newspaper accounts of the crime at the Sand Pits. When Carter suggested this was unusual considering the media attention given the incident, he answered, "Have you ever tried to get a newspaper at Argentia?"

The surprise witness learned of the episode when he visited Doane two weeks before the trial. He told the court that Doane told him about her arrest and said the police were trying to pin the crime on her. When he left her he went to his office and reviewed his notes and records. June 25 was an important date and he wanted to accurately recall his activities that night.

The following Friday he returned to Doane's apartment and told her that he had reviewed his records and was absolutely certain she was with him that night. Doane said she didn't know what the police were trying to do. She said, first they said it happened on June 25 then they changed it and said it happened June 26.

The next day Maloney took his evidence to Sam Hawkins.

Hawkins subpoenaed Maloney to testify for the defence. His evidence was simple and to the point. Linda Doane could not have been involved because she was in his company from 10:30 p.m. to 1:00 a.m. on the night in question. The offence allegedly occurred at about 1:00 a.m.

Maloney then went on to recount his activities that night. He told the court he picked up Linda Doane between 10:30 and 11:00 and drove to the Pioneer Restaurant on Portugal Cove Road. "We were served by a cute little blond," he added.

Continuing his testimony he explained, "When we left the Pioneer, we drove to Winsor Lake. It was about 1:30 when I brought her home." Under cross-examination by Carter he expressed certainty about the date. Maloney explained that the date stood out in his mind because it was the day before he went to Argentia.

The defence witness noted that his job took him all over the island. Early on the day of June 25 he was on Bell Island and he told the court, "I have the time sheets to prove it."

Maloney had gone to Bell Island to give an estimate on a paint job. He returned to the city that night. The witness testified he had an appointment to meet Linda Doane at Bell's on Duckworth Street. She did not turn up so he went to her apartment.

When the prosecutor suggested he was put up to testifying by the accused he answered, "I wasn't asked by Miss Doane to come here. I went to Miss Doane and told her it was the night she was with me. I can't be wrong. I remember it was the next day that I went to Argentia."

Carter stated, "You are aware that Eli Dooley identified Linda Doane as the person he drove to the Sand Pits."

Maloney replied, "Yes, but he is either mistaken or lying."

Carter asked, "How long have you known Linda Doane?"

"Two or three years," the witness answered.

"Did you know if she was married?" questioned the prosecutor.

"I never asked her if she was married or single," replied the witness.

Interest in the trial reached its peak on the day Linda Doane was scheduled to take the stand. Spectators lined up outside the courthouse hoping to get inside to witness the unfolding drama. Over 100 people had to be turned away.

When Doane took the stand, a hush fell over the courtroom. Many spectators leaned ahead in their seats attempting to catch every word spoken by the attractive and smartly dressed witness.

In her testimony Doane recalled her activities on the twenty-fifty and early morning hours of the twenty-sixth. She told the court she was in the company of Mr. Maloney that night from 10:30 p.m. to after 1:00 a.m. They went to the Pioneer Drive-In Restaurant on Portugal Cove Road. She recalled that when they left the Pioneer they went to Winsor Lake and then Maloney took her home. It was after 1:00 a.m.

When Hawkins questioned her about the arrest and questioning by the RCMP she answered, "Coady was all show and tried to let me know he was hot."

"Did you complain about the police lineup," asked Hawkins.

"Yes, I did. I complained about the girls in the line-up. One was like she was drunk. She couldn't stay still. They were having fun. Constable Coady was having fun.

"All the girls in the lineup had been drinking and they were falling all over the place." The witness noted that she was sober and the only one in the lineup wearing a bandanna.

Hawkins interjected, "Did you compare to the girls in the line-up?"

"No, no, no — good lord! No!" exclaimed Doane.

"What type of girls were they?" asked Hawkins.

Doane was quick to reply, "Street girls. I saw them before in the company of Negroes."

The defence then delved into her alibi for the hours of the crime. Hawkins began, "Did you know Eli Dooley?"

The witness answered, "Yes. I knew of him. I was never taken to his car any time let alone Tuesday night."

Hawkins queried, "Did you go to the Sand Pits?"

"No Mr. Hawkins that is definitely not my territory," shot back Linda Doane. Throughout her testimony she denied any knowledge of the dead babies.

"Is Mr. Maloney's evidence facts?" Hawkins asked.

The witness answered, "Yes. They have had ample time to check on it."

Hawkins continued his questioning, "What kind of man is Maloney?"

"A lovely, man," replied Doane. "A very nice man."

The defence lawyer then told the witness that the charge she was facing was a very serious charge. He suggested that either some of the evidence was astounding or "somebody is mistaken in the time."

After a brief hesitation Hawkins looked straight at the witness and asked, "Did you commit the offence for which you are accused?"

Linda Doane was firm in her reply, "No. I did not. I know absolutely nothing about it."

Satisfied with the answer, Hawkins commented, "I have no further questions Your Honour."

The crown prosecutor then began his cross-examination of the accused. He began by having the accused detail some of her personal background. In response Linda Doane said she had come to Newfoundland in 1953 following her marriage break up. She came here because she thought she would like it. Her husband was also living here but his presence had no influence on her decision.

The prosecution then asked Doane if she had any money on her when arrested and where she got it. Hawkins objected, arguing that it questioned the character of the witness.

"Do you have an occupation," asked Carter. Doane responded, "I sell dry goods and I run my own business modelling clothes and buying and selling them." She added that she had a legal separation and received a monthly allowance from her husband.

When Linda Doane first arrived in St. John's she lived in various hotels including the Balsam. She eventually moved to a third floor apartment at 92 Queen's Road.

Carter asked Doane, "How long have you known Maloney ?"

"Three years," replied the witness.
Carter: "Was he married?"
Doane: "I don't know."
Carter: "Where did he live?"
Doane: "I don't know."
Carter: "Do you know his telephone number?"
Doane: "No."

Carter: "You told the court you saw Maloney about every ten days and you didn't know if he was married, his address or telephone number?"

Doane: "I never asked him."

The prosecutor then turned his attention to Doane's knowledge of the cabbie. "Do you know Eli Dooley?" asked Carter.

"I know him to see him," answered Doane.

"Ever speak to him?" asked Carter.

"Yes," Doane said, "down on Duckworth Street sometime in 1955. He had three Negroes in the car and he asked me if I was interested in going for a drive. Two or three times after he asked me and I said no. I asked him why he asked me? He told me he had heard things. I said don't bother me."

Carter asked, "Did you feel offended?"

Doane answered, "At first I did, then I thought, hell, let the Islanders have their day." At this point Doane became irritated and turned to Carter saying, "You're just like Coady."

The prosecutor continued his efforts to poke holes in Doane's testimony. To every question put to her about going to the Sand Pits in Dooley's car, Doane denied any knowledge.

Carter continued his questioning, "Were you disturbed when the police went to see you?"

Doane: "No, I was not annoyed. I just wondered why it was me."

Carter: "Were you disturbed when Dooley identified you?

Doane: "Yes, I was getting disturbed. He had spoiled my day."

When Carter questioned her about the statement she gave RCMP which conflicted with her testimony in court Doane did not hesitate to answer. She said, "Coady made it all up himself and I signed it."

The prosecutor asked, "Did you make an objection?"

"Yes, but I signed it," answered Doane.

Carter questioned why Doane had not mentioned Maloney in her statement to police. She said, "The police asked me about it. I said yes, I was on the Portugal Cove Road and went to the Pioneer."

The prosecutor then read the statement she gave police. It stated she went home 11:45 on the twenty-fifty and did not see anyone she knew. She had lost her garbage pail sometime in December.

Doane interrupted, "These are statements taken from the two of them. You have a combination of both statements. I did not feel at any time that I had to say anything." (Police had taken two statements from Doane.)

Carter shot back, "Wasn't it in your interest to tell the truth?"

Doane replied, "What difference does it make. I signed the statement without reading it."

Carter asked, "Do you sign things without reading them?"

Doane: "When I'm annoyed, yes. I didn't mention Maloney. I didn't think I had to. If they chose to make that mistake themselves that's their business. They knew I was down at the Pioneer at the time, just ask them."

Carter: "Surely, knowing this was such a serious charge you were suspected of, couldn't you remember your movements?"

Doane: "I didn't have to tell them about Mr. Maloney. No, I had no intention of mentioning it. I could have faced this myself without Mr. Maloney."

The prosecutor asked Doane about her meeting with Maloney on July 1, a week after the crime. The witness said she told him of the charges then. She recalled, "I said Jimmy have you heard the news about the infant they found in the Sand Pits, they have that pinned on me!"

Doane recalled that they were together several times after that, and on one occasion she told him the police were changing the date of the charge from the twenty-fifth to the twenty-sixth. She commented, "We had been talking about the twenty-fifth now its the twenty-sixth. I don't know what the hell they are doing." The night of the twenty-fifth suddenly became important to Maloney.

According to Doane he asked her, "Wasn't that the night we were out to the Pioneer. The next thing I knew he had been to see my lawyer."

Carter interjected, "Wasn't that the first time you remembered the twenty-fifth.

Doane answered, "No. But I felt I didn't have to say so."

Carter challenged Doane, "In other words you told the police a lie."

Doane said, "It was not a lie."

At this point the defence objected asking, "Is this questioning necessary?"

Doane again showed her irritation and commented, "I know Mr. Hawkins — what he is trying to do. Coady was not interested in getting facts. He was only interested in getting me before a magistrate without representation. He's a little Hitler without the moustache." She told the court the statement she gave was for Wednesday not for Tuesday and she signed it, and ". . . thought no more about it."

Carter's final question was, "Do you know any reason why Eli Dooley would tell that story if it was not true?"

"To collect the witness fee," concluded Linda Doane. The defence had concluded its case. The next stage was the summation by the defence and prosecution.

Hawkins began his summation by noting that his client was charged with an unusual crime. He argued that the offence in question dealt with a person trying to dispose of their own child. "However," he explained to the jury, "the Crown made no attempt to prove the child belonged to Linda Doane."

The defence lawyer reviewed the trial evidence and concluded the case revolved around the question of identity. He said, "The evidence makes it clear and beyond all reasonable doubt, that the guilt of the accused resolves itself into the question of identity. The evidence of the prosecution has resolved itself into mistaken identity or something bordering on deliberate lies."

The only evidence connecting Doane to the crime, according to Hawkins, was Dooley's testimony. He noted, "All police information is from Dooley only. They moved fast and they stepped in where angels fear to tread."

Turning his attention to defence evidence, Hawkins told the jury that, "The accused completely denied the story. The court has no choice but to dismiss the charge." He added that the evidence of Maloney was enough to acquit Doane. Hawkins said, "If there is any doubt to believe Dooley, there is less reason to doubt Maloney."

The defence reviewed the evidence of Dr. Ross. "There is no motive," said Hawkins. He explained, "The Doctor's evidence showed the accused did not have a baby within the four weeks before the examination." Hawkins also pounded away at the reliability of the police lineup.

Spectators listened attentively as Sam Hawkins concluded his summation. "To convict by the evidence of one crown witness is dangerous when there is any indication that the witness is an accomplice," warned Hawkins. He continued, "The whole question is of identification. I don't know whose mistake it is, but I feel that the evidence demands an acquittal."

It was now Harry Carter's turn to try to sway the jury. Carter portrayed Dooley as a credible witness who should be believed. He said, "Dooley's evidence was from a man who was there and saw what happened."

The prosecutor challenged the defence's claim that Dooley was possibly an accomplice whose testimony was not reliable. He told the jury, "There is no evidence Dooley was an accomplice. It's nonsense to suggest that this man would bring in such evidence."

Carter pointed out to the jury that Dooley had testified that Doane told him at the crime scene that she had lost her garbage pail. He felt this added to Dooley's credibility because Doane had told police in her signed statement that she had lost her garbage pail. At this point, Doane interjected, "Your Honour, I never had a garbage pail."

"But, you did tell police that you did," shot back Carter.

The prosecutor then went on to deal with the unexpected alibi evidence and the surprise appearance of the witness Maloney. He emphasized that, "The defence of alibi ought to be introduced at the earliest point as a rule of expediency."

Carter reminded the jury that the accused made no attempt to tell the police she had an alibi. He added, "Whatever the woman says, it would be hard to believe that anyone charged with such a serious offence would not take it seriously. At the time the statement was given she deliberately lied to the RCMP. She was not under oath. It is difficult to believe that she was with Maloney. Why didn't she mention it?"

At this point defence lawyer, Sam Hawkins asked to speak. He told the court, "Whether the alibi is true I don't know. But on the question of waiting until the last moment to bring it to court, that was my advice. I advised her to say nothing to the police."

With the summations of both the defence and the prosecution concluded, attention focused on Magistrate Hugh O'Neill. He began his address to the jury by reading the charge. He read, ". . . that on June 26 at the Sand Pits the accused did unlawfully dispose of the body of a dead infant by attempting to burn to conceal the birth of a child."

O'Neill then commented upon the evidence. He noted the question of identification in the lineup was not very important because, "Dooley said he knew the complainant before."

He drew the jury's attention to the accused's denial of the crime. O'Neill said, "Linda Doane testified that she had no knowledge of the event." The judge also reviewed the evidence of Dr. Ross which showed the accused had not given birth to a child.

After reviewing the alibi evidence he drew attention to a piece of evidence that could have been helpful. He referred to the accused's written statement that she had lost her garbage pail. This, he explained, could give credibility to Dooley's evidence. However, he suggested the possibility that Dooley's evidence could have been influenced by police questioning.

The magistrate commented on a second piece of evidence that could be considered. He said the tenants living next to Doane had asked her that night if she could smell gas? O'Neill said, "If the bodies were in the house and there were no odours the accused may have felt it was time to get rid of them."

Finally, Magistrate Hugh O'Neill gave the statement long awaited by the accused. He concluded, "In view of the evidence I have no choice but to acquit the accused."

Linda Doane thanked her lawyer, tossed her hair back and smiled at police officers as she left the court room. The trial was over but the crime not solved. Two murders had been committed and nobody has ever been charged.

The Evening Telegram hit the justice system hard in its editorial the next day which claimed the case had been bungled.

The editorial read:

> "To say that the prosecution bungled the Linda Doane trial would be an understatement. They brought the woman to court and tried to convict her on the lone evidence of a taxi driver. They failed to follow up several important lines of evidence — one of which was pointed out to them by the Magistrate in his judgement. They left great ques-

tions, the most important questions in the case, as a matter of fact, completely untouched.

"The babies whose burned bodies were found in the Sand Pits were evidently murdered. They were certainly born alive, and the medical experts did not believe that they died of natural causes. They were apparently not a twin. It would seem that somewhere in the background there must be two females — neither of whom is Linda Doane — who gave birth to children and then murdered them. The person who burned the bodies in the Sand Pits may have been acting merely as the agent of the murderers.

"To begin with, Miss Doane was tried for much the lesser crime in the case, disposing of a dead body is a trivial offence when compared with murder. But it appears that the police and the Department of the Attorney General would have been quite happy to 'secure a conviction,' as they like to put it, on this lesser charge, than to write off the whole case as closed.

"If nothing else was proved beyond question in this astonishing trial, it was reasonably well established that Miss Doane had not recently given birth to a baby. What, then, are we to assume about the identity of the dead babies? Did the police make any effort to discover who they were, or did the evidence volunteered by taximan Dooley sweep them so completely off their feet that they lost interest in all other aspects of the case?

"It has been said before that once the 'state' brings a suspect to court and completes a trial it considers a case automatically closed. Once a person has been tried and found innocent, the guilty person or persons can breathe easy, for there will be no further police investigation. This is due in part to the fact that the 'state' continues to assume the guilt of its suspects, even when they are cleared by the courts, but also in part to the fact that the 'state' feels it has cleared itself with the general public. The demand that a case be reopened and further investigated, once it has been tried, is rare.

"But in a case of a bungled prosecution such as this we feel that the demand is amply justified. We have not the slightest reason to suppose that the police made any effort whatsoever to discover the killers of the babies whose bodies were found in the Sand Pits. We should like some assurance that they feel it their duty to do so, in fact that they feel called upon to investigate all the unexplained aspects of this case. The form of murder known as infanticide is not a respectable practice in our society. It is against the law. We should expect this fact to be generally recognized, and not be content with substitute charges and substitute trials concerned with the disposal of the bodies."

The editorial fell on deaf ears. Time marched on and memories faded. The same questions that confronted police on the day the bodies were discovered remain unanswered almost forty years later. The murder of two children remains an unsolved crime.

NEWFOUNDLAND CONNECTIONS

FOILED KIDNAPPING

IN JUNE, 1976, the fourteen-year-old daughter of John Craig Eaton — of Eaton's of Canada Ltd. — was rescued from a kidnapping attempt by a Newfoundland member of the Toronto Metropolitan Police. During the dramatic confrontation with the kidnapper, Constable Shawn Clarke put his own life on the line.

This life or death situation for Clarke and young Signy Eaton began in the early morning hours of June 15, 1976. Constable Clarke, a tall powerfully built man, was on general police duties with his partner Constable David Linney that day. At 1:54 a.m. they responded to what seemed to be a routine call, to check on a complaint of a prowler in the area of the Eaton residence.

Clarke explained why he felt the call was just routine. He said, "It was a routine call . . . usually nothing happens, but we hurried to the area to check it out." While proceeding to the Eaton home, Clarke speculated the prowler was likely someone out getting night worms for a fishing trip. Toronto has a city by-law prohibiting picking of worms at night in city parks. Because of this, people looking for fishing bait frequently go out at night and search the lawns of neighbours.

The two officers received a second call on their police radio which convinced Clarke the prowler was just someone looking for worms. The call noted that a neighbour said he saw a man with a hat, a flashlight and a stick walking near the Eaton home.

Within minutes the police pulled into the Eaton driveway and using their flashlights immediately initiated a search of the grounds. Constable Clarke commented, "I checked the back of the residence and my partner checked the front. Everything seemed OK. We were about to leave when I decided to speak to the people in the house, and make sure they were alright."

After unsuccessfully trying to get an answer at the front door, the twenty-four-year-old Newfoundlander walked to the back of the house. Glancing toward a side window he noticed a flashlight in one of the bedrooms. He approached the back door, and found it open. Instinctively Clarke sensed something was wrong.

The police officer responded calmly to the situation. He asked his partner to call for a back-up. Meanwhile, he decided to enter the house through the basement door in an effort to prevent any intruder from leaving the house. Constable Clarke described what happened: "I opened the basement door and saw a man standing three feet away from me . . . holding onto a young girl." The kidnapper was pointing a high-powered military rifle (an M-1 carbine) directly at the Newfoundlander's chest.

Clarke drew his 38 revolver from its holster but the kidnapper ordered him to drop the weapon. Clarke recalled that the basement was dark but the man knew he (Clarke) had the gun. Twice the kidnapper demanded Clarke drop his gun but the cop held his ground.

Constable Clarke said, "I was thinking about the girl's life so I couldn't fire." Instead he kept his revolver pointed at the intruder and slowly backed out of the basement. Outside he pressed against the side of the house. Meanwhile, the kidnapper emerged and dropped the girl as he stepped outside the door. She ran back into the house. Clarke sensed that the kidnapper was only concerned with getting away. When he made a dash across the yard, Clarke followed in hot pursuit. The kidnapper clutched his rifle as he ran.

Clarke recalled firing six bullets at the kidnapper. It was dark and each shot missed. Clarke said, "He got over a fence and I could hear his footsteps so I continued the pursuit."

The constable ordered a four block area to be sealed off and the Emergency Tactic Force was called in to assist. By dawn the police had forty-seven-year-old Ernest Carron of Montreal in custody for the kidnapping attempt. Carron was turned over to Constable Clarke, who took him to the police station for questioning.

However, when police investigators returned to the Eaton mansion to search for clues they were surprised by what they found. In an upstairs bedroom, the intruder had confined thirty-nine-year-old John Eaton and his wife Sherry.

When Carron first entered the house he took John and Sherry at gunpoint to the upstairs room. There he tied and gagged his captives. He then searched the house until he found the Eaton's young daughter, Signy. Pointing the gun at her he threatened to shoot if she did not do as she was told. He was in the final stage of his crime, leaving the house with his victim, when his scheme was thwarted by the Newfoundland police officer.

Clarke had a long-time ambition to be a police officer. He tried to join both the RCMP and the RNC but was not accepted. He then applied to the Toronto Metropolitan Police and earned a place on the force. At the time of the kidnapping attempt Clarke had been on the force for two years, and this marked the first occasion on which he'd needed to use his gun. The life-threatening confrontation with danger did not dampen Clarke's spirit or love for police work. He commented, "This is one job that I put in one hundred per cent effort and I enjoy every shift."

IT SHOCKED NEW YORK

THE DISCOVERY of a butchered twelve-year-old child in a vacant tenement lot at the Bronx, New York on July 10, 1910 sparked a city-wide mobilization of police investigators, which led to the arrest of a young Newfoundlander.

Due to its brutality, the murder shocked New Yorkers and Newfoundlanders alike. The girl had been badly beaten, her hair was chopped off and there were repeated stab wounds over her upper body. New Yorker's were in a lynching mood.

Police moved swiftly to solve the crime and in less than forty-eight hours had a young Newfoundlander, Ernest Hottville, behind bars. Hottville had moved to New York from St. John's, Newfoundland some years earlier with his family. He worked in the big city as a labourer. He lived in the same neighbourhood as the victim and matched the detailed eye-witness description of the man last seen with the girl.

At the precinct police station the young Newfoundlander was subjected to an intensive and gruelling interrogation at the hands of investigators. Police had searched Hottville for evidence but found nothing, ". . . of a suspicious nature." Apart from proclaiming his innocence, Hottville would not answer any of the police questions. He refused even to tell his address. Police were sure they had the killer.

Early next morning, with the Bronx courtroom filled with reporters, the accused monster killer was paraded in handcuffs to face the judge, where he was officially charged with the murder of Julia Connors. That evening New York papers reported the arrest and charging of the Newfoundlander. Newspapers described the killing as, "... a crime that passes comprehension."

A Grand Jury was immediately convened and the

wheels of justice moved rapidly. Within days the Grand Jury unanimously voted in favour of an "indictment of murder in the first degree." However, it was not Ernest Hottville who was indicted.

An astonishing turn of events occurred during the second day of the court hearing, which sent reporters scrambling out the doors to break the news. A distressed and despondent Hottville suddenly sat up alert and smiled at his favourable turn of fate.

The New York papers on July 16 described the episode: "Samuel Swartz, father of Nathan Swartz, a young hanger-on of pugilism who had been sought in connection with the crime, admitted to the Grand Jury that his son had confessed to him that he was guilty of killing the girl." This evidence was corroborated by another witness, Mrs. Frances Alexander, the sister of Nathan Swartz.

Mrs. Alexander's repetition of the story of the crime told to her by her brother, was detailed, explicit and telling in its revelation of horror. The witness testified that her brother had told her that he had met Julia Connors on Saturday night and asked her to take a pair of opera glasses to his home, which was just across the hall from the vacant flat where the murder was committed. The young man said he followed the girl, and at the top of the stairs pushed her into the flat and attempted to assault her. The child screamed, according to the story of Mrs. Alexander, and then Nathan said he plunged his pocket knife into her. She continued to scream, the witness testified, and Nathan stabbed her until she finally fell and then he plunged the knife into her breast near the heart. Then Julia remained still.

Nathan went across the hall to his own home, the witness continued, and procured the box in which the body was found. He placed the still living child into this box, after cutting off her hair, put the box on the dumbwaiter and let it slide to the bottom.

Mrs. Alexander told the Grand Jury that Nathan said

he went to the cellar and took the unconscious child from the dumb waiter and laid her in the cellar. He then went home and went to sleep. Early the next morning (Sunday) he took the girl, still alive, into the lot where she was found.

The witness said she threw the youth out of her house when she heard the tale. He then went to his father's place of business where, according to evidence given by his father, he told the same story.

While records were not clear on what happened to Nathan Swartz, it was locally believed that he served a life sentence in a New York prison. Hottville, walked out of the court room exonerated. For a short while his was a household name in New York City. But in time the travesty of justice committed against this young Newfoundlander was forgotten. The memory of the Hottville case has long since disappeared from the public mind.

THE MURDER OF MONA JOHNSON

THE REPULSIVE AND MACABRE SLAYING of forty-nine-year-old Mona Johnson at Little Catalina shocked her neighbours and friends. The trial of her killer absolutely amazed them. Newfoundlanders have rarely been subjected to such a ghastly and despicable a crime; our courts have rarely seen such a bizarre murder trial as the one that followed.

This peculiar justice story began about 2:00 a.m. on February 4, 1976. Two employees of the Department of Transportation and Communication, Clarence Murphy and Wallace Trask — both of Elliston, Trinity Bay — were in the vicinity of Mona Johnson's. Mrs. Johnson lived alone in a small bungalow on a side road in Little Catalina; her nearest neighbour was three hundred feet down the road. Suddenly flames burst out from the back area of the Johnson residence; both men rushed to a nearby house to call for help.

At 2:10 a.m. the call was received by the Chief of the Volunteer Fire Department in the community, Ancel Johnson. Within fifteen minutes the volunteer fire brigade was at the scene battling the flames.

The Chief knew Mona lived alone and he looked around to see if she had escaped the inferno. There was not a sign of Mona Johnson and the neighbours had not seen her. As they watched the flames engulf the home they hoped and prayed that Mona had spent the night with relatives or friends.

The fire brigade fought the blaze until they got it under control at 4:30 a.m. At 6:30 a.m., while searching the ruins, they discovered the body of Mona Johnson, lying face down on the bedroom floor. Constable Edward Dunn, the first police officer on the scene, was with Chief Johnson when they turned over the body to make an identification. What they saw instantly alerted them to the fact that foul play had been involved in the affair.

The fire chief and police officer had noticed what appeared to be plastic coated wire around the wrists and throat of the victim. She was partially naked and covered in debris. Constable Dunn noted that her arms were spread out from her body and there was wire around her right wrist and throat. Police wasted no time in launching a murder investigation. The area was immediately sealed off and a search of the ruins conducted to gather evidence.

Meanwhile, an investigative team began the long and laborious job of seeking witnesses and evidence that would lead to the arrest of the person or persons responsible for the killing. The police learned that after Mona Johnson was divorced she had lived for a short time with relatives at Little Catalina. Police went to the home of these relatives to gather background information on the victim. They had no idea when they approached Mrs. Anne Chaulk that a person in the house would soon set them on the right path towards arresting the person responsible for the crime.

While police discussed Mona Johnson with Anne Chaulk, Andrew Scott Reid, Chaulk's grandson, was in an upstairs room listening to their conversation. Reid came down from his room and offered to help the police. He told Corporal Green that he had been in the vicinity of Mona's home at about 1:00 a.m. that morning. He claimed he'd seen a dark coloured car in her driveway, adding that he had not seen the car before.

Corporal Green took notes on the information and left the Chaulks to question other witnesses. However, several people questioned by the police contradicted Reid's story which made Corporal Green suspicious. He returned to question Reid further and invited him to go to RCMP offices at Bonavista for further questioning. Andrew Reid agreed.

Green later recalled that Reid expressed concern over what people in the community might think if they saw him with the police. The police officer noted also that Andrew was concerned that people would not believe what he had to say. When Green suggested that Reid take a polygraph test Reid agreed that it would be a good idea.

By 12:20 p.m. that day Andrew Scott Reid was at RCMP offices in Bonavista. He gave police two statements which were similar to the verbal statement he had given earlier that day at his grandmother's home.

Reid told police that the night before he was in a car drinking with friends. He said, "We bought a dozen beer and then sat in a parked car and drank and sang songs." He claimed he had three or four beers before the group broke up and went home. Reid said his friends dropped him off near Mona's house at about 1:00 a.m.

Reid told police that he considered going in to visit his cousin (Mona) but after seeing the dark blue car in the driveway decided against it. Instead he walked home and went to bed.

During the interrogation, Staff Sergeant Vince O'Donnell, in charge of the investigation, arrived at the police offices. He instructed Corporal Green to ask Reid about the clothes he wore on the night of the fire and to explain the scratch on his nose. When confronted with this line of questioning, Reid's mood changed and he asked to use the telephone.

Reid agreed to give the sergeant a written statement. It was 9:15 a.m., February 6. He told police that he was walking home past Mona's during the early morning on February 4. He had been dropped off near there in a car by the friends he had been drinking with earlier that night.

Reid said it was a cold night and he decided he would drop in to visit his cousin, Mona Johnson. Mona answered the knock on the door and Reid claimed he asked her if he could come inside because it was cold out. She invited him inside. When he was in the house he claimed he saw "Rose," a girl he had at one time been engaged to, holding his son in her arms.

Reid told police, "I asked her if she still loved me." He added she began putting a plastic shoe horn down his son's throat and said, "This is how much I love you." His statement said he then strangled her with a telephone cord and set fire to the house by lighting the clothing on the bed. He told Power that he then hid his blood-stained clothing in an outdoor toilet.

Reid described Rose as a girl he met in Toronto about five years earlier. He commented, "We were engaged. She broke it off. It was the worst thing that ever happened to me."

The police again suggested to Reid that he take the lie detector test and he agreed. O'Donnell put the wheels in motion immediately to arrange a polygraph test for the suspect. Accommodations were arranged at the Albatross Hotel, Gander and Sergeant John Neil, a polygraph expert from Halifax, was flown there to administer the testing. Two officers from the General Investigating Service of the RCMP, Corporal Ed McHugh and Sergeant Larry Power, were assigned to take the suspect to Gander. Corporal John Green and Constable Fred Graham were assigned to guard the prisoner at Gander.

Andrew Reid was a musician and played with a local band at Little Catalina. During the trip to Gander on February 6 Reid was calm and in a casual mood. His concern appeared not to be with the murder investigation but with a dance at Little Catalina that night. He expressed concern to the police officers over the possibility of being late for the dance. When Corporal McHugh asked him how he got the scratch on his nose he replied, "I got that playing with my dog."

The police and suspect arrived at the Albatross at 5:30 p.m. They waited in the lobby for the arrival of the polygraph expert who showed up shortly after 6 p.m. When Sergeant Neil went into a room to set up the polygraph machine Reid's casual mood changed. He began to display nervousness. Reid told McHugh, "If they ask me certain questions I'm not going to answer them."

McHugh asked, "What type of questions?"

Reid answered, "For instance, if they say 'Did you kill or murder Mona?' I'm not going to answer."

Corporal McHugh noted the change in Reid's behaviour. He commented, "He was not casual anymore. He was showing signs of worry and concern. From his questions and appearance I formed the opinion Reid was responsible for Mrs. Johnson's death."

McHugh was concerned that the agitated mood of the suspect might adversely affect the polygraph test. He asked Sergeant Power, ". . . to rush things because of the change in the accused." From past experience he had learned that people taking the polygraph should be as calm as possible.

Sergeant Power told McHugh that police had found a parka and shirt in an outhouse near Reid's home that they suspected belonged to Andrew Scott Reid. They were covered in blood stains. Power explained the blood stains were similar to the blood of Mona Johnson.

Police moved quickly to administer the polygraph test. Corporal McHugh took Reid to Sergeant Neil's room shortly after 6 p.m. and the testing went on until 9:15 p.m. At that time Sergeant Neil emerged from the room to inform McHugh that Reid had confessed to the crime and wanted to speak with him. McHugh described the mood of the accused at that time: "He was more upset than he had been before and from his appearance it was plain to see he had been crying."

His first words to McHugh were, "You knew it all the time, but I couldn't tell you." Corporal McHugh noted that the accused was an intelligent person. He asked Reid if he knew he would now be charged with murder. Reid sobbed and answered, "Yes." The investigator then read to the accused the police caution and placed him under arrest.

McHugh asked Reid what he did with the clothes he wore the night of the murder. He answered, "I put the parka and shirt down an old toilet." The officer then asked if Reid had sex with Mona. Reid was irritated over the question and replied, "No! No! I never touched her. I never touched her."

Reid was held in custody at Gander overnight and returned to Bonavista the next morning. During the ride to Bonavista McHugh asked Reid to point out where he had hidden the parka and shirt. He directed the police to an outhouse near his grandmother's at Little Catalina. Reid was not aware that police had already recovered the clothing.

While in Little Catalina Reid lay down on the back seat to avoid being seen by anyone in the community. He told the police he did not want to be seen and he remarked, "I thought and I thought but I can't figure out why I did it."

During the drive to Bonavista Reid began discussing what happened that night. He said, "I had to get rid of her. I took the cord off the telephone. I cut it with a knife. I hit her. There was blood all over the place. There was blood on my clothes. I knew I had to get rid of her. When I tied her up I didn't think she was dead but she didn't move. I got the wire and tied it around her neck to make sure she was dead."

As sort of an afterthought Reid commented, "Would you believe I don't know how I got the scratch on my nose? I had to make up the story that the dog did it. I had to tell you something."

On February 7 in court at Bonavista, Andrew Scott Reid was charged with non-capital murder in connection with the death of Mona Johnson. He was remanded to the Hospital for Mental and Nervous Diseases for a psychological examination to determine if he was fit to stand trial.

Following a ten day assessment Reid was brought to Magistrate's Court at St. John's. Magistrate Hugh O'Neill listened attentively as doctors explained the results of the assessment. He then ruled that the accused was fit to stand trial. A preliminary hearing was scheduled for March 25 at Bonavista. Robert Wells appeared in court on behalf of Reid and Barry Hill represented the Crown.

St. John's lawyer, Randy Earle, filled in for Robert Wells at the preliminary hearing. At the conclusion of the hearing the judge set June 2 as the date for the accused to be arraigned in Supreme Court. At the arraignment Reid pleaded not guilty and Justice Arthur Mifflin set the trial date for June 14, two weeks later.

By trial date Reid gave the appearances of being calm and in control. The twenty-six year old, blond-haired fish plant worker sat attentively in the prisoner's box flanked by two RCMP officers. He wore a sports coat, checkered shirt and dark slacks. Occasionally he jotted down notes and sometimes glanced at his wife Viola who sat among the spectators.

Crown prosecutor, Barry Hill told the court he would present evidence showing that Andrew Scott Reid had gagged, bound, sexually assaulted and strangled Mona Johnson with a telephone wire. Mr. Hill said the accused then set the house in a blaze in a desperate attempt to destroy the evidence. He said he would call expert witnesses to present evidence connecting the accused to the crime.

The defence attempted to stop the Crown from introducing statements given by the accused to police as evidence. Reid had given five statements. Three of these were written statements and two were given orally. These statements said that Reid believed he was killing a former girl friend when he strangled Mona Johnson. A Voir Dire, which lasted five days, determined that all statements to police by the accused were admissible. The Crown would call thirty-seven witnesses.

Meanwhile the defence would rest its case on one witness. The accused himself, Andrew Scott Reid. Reid would deny killing Mona Johnson and startle the court with a bizarre account of what happened.

Sixteen-year-old Maxwell Rumbolt, who gave evidence for the Crown at the preliminary hearing, accidentally drowned before the trial date. His testimony was therefore read into court records by Mr. Hill. The Crown was developing its story as to the circumstances surrounding the death of the victim and suggested the fire had started in the bedroom where the body was discovered.

Maxwell Rumbolt lived down the road from Mrs. Johnson. He was up late on February 4 watching the late show on television. A sudden light piercing the darkness outside caught his attention. Rumbolt went to the window and identified the source of the light as flames coming from the house of Mona Johnson. He testified that these flames were coming from the rear of the Johnson house where the victim's bedroom was located.

Another Crown witness indicated that the victim had been receiving harassing telephone calls. Fred Rumbolt, a neighbour who often dated Mona Johnson, testified that he could not make contact with Mrs. Johnson on February 3. He said that at 10:00 a.m. he talked with her by phone and she told him she had the flu and was not feeling well. Later that day he decided to pay a visit to Mrs. Johnson. He went to her door at 5:30 p.m. and knocked unsuccessfully several times before leaving. He tried to gain entry but discovered the door had been locked from the inside. At 9:30 p.m. he tried again to reach Mrs. Johnson by phone. There was no answer.

When cross-examined by Mr. Hill, Rumbolt said it was strange for the door to be locked from the inside. He added that it was also unusual for her not to reply to his telephone call at 9:30 p.m. He explained that he felt she must have gone out.

Because Mona had been receiving harassing telephone calls she and Fred used a special system for telephoning each other. Rumbolt explained the system to the court. He said he would call her and let the phone ring once, then hang up. Mona, then would return his call. Mr. Rumbolt testified that he was up late that night awaiting his son's return from Bonavista. He said at 3:00 a.m. he noticed flames coming from Mona's house.

The autopsy was performed by Dr. Peter Markesteyn, forensic pathologist at the General Hospital, St. John's. The autopsy report showed that Mona Johnson had been badly beaten about the face and strangled with a plastic covered telephone wire. The plastic covering melted in the fire but the wire remained around the woman's throat and hands.

Lucy Bishop, an expert with the RCMP Crime Lab at Sackville, New Brunswick, testified that the victim was gagged, bound, sexually assaulted and strangled with a telephone cord.

Dr. Markesteyn observed that the body had been exposed to fire and smoke and there was plastic coated wire around the wrist, neck and part of the mouth. He suggested that it appeared to be two cords around the victim's throat.

Some traces of textile found on the wire in the mouth brought the pathologist to the conclusion that a gag had been applied to the victim's mouth. He concluded that death was caused by strangulation because there was no soot in the woman's air passages and therefore no evidence she was breathing while the fire was in progress.

When cross-examined by Mr. Hill, Dr. Markesteyn explained that it is extremely rare for a person to suffocate from being gagged unless the tongue is pushed into the back of the throat. He said Mrs. Johnson's tongue was protruding through her teeth and he did not believe the gag had caused her death.

Commenting on evidence that the victim was bleeding from the neck the witness explained, "This was the result of a force being applied and sustained to her neck. I reached the conclusion that the application of the wire around her neck caused strangulation."

The doctor could not say for certain if a repulsive head injury had been caused before or after the death. He noted, "There was a large hole in the victim's skull and her brain was visible. I could not reach a conclusion based on the x-rays and examinations, on whether it was caused by something that occurred before the death. It is not uncommon for such an injury to be caused by the extreme heat of a fire. The x-rays showed there were no other bones broken."

The pathologist told the court that Mona Johnson had been raped before death. He stated that, ". . . sexual intercourse did take place prior to death. Not by mutual consent." He explained that the elastic material found on the victim's legs was apparently her underclothing and it had been there before the fire began. He concluded his testimony stating that he had taken specimens from the victim's vaginal area and blood samples which were forwarded to the RCMP Crime Lab at Sackville, N.B.

Police expert Lucy Bishop told the court that the blood stains on Andrew Reid's clothing were similar to Mona Johnson's blood. The crime lab had also determined from the victim's blood samples that she had not been drinking alcoholic beverages. There were no traces of alcohol in the victim's body.

Sergeant John Neill, who administered the polygraph test on the accused, testified that during the process Reid broke down and cried before confessing to strangling Mona Johnson and setting fire to her house. He told the court that Reid had volunteered to take the polygraph. The witness said that he explained to Reid how the polygraph worked and reminded him that he did not have to take it. Reid said he wanted to take it and Sergeant Neill read him the police caution.

Sergeant Neill described Reid's mood while being tested. He said, "Reid appeared rational but concerned." He testified that Reid was, ". . . a cunning individual because he thought out the answers to all his questions."

During the session, Reid told the police sergeant that he had not slept since the death of Mona Johnson. When the conversation touched on his relationship with a former girl friend he had met five years previously in Toronto, Reid became upset. He told Sergeant Neill, "We were engaged but she broke it off."

The accused then went on to give a bizarre account of a recurring dream he was having. He claimed he had dreams of his son choking on a piece of plastic shoehorn that someone was putting down his throat.

The police officer noted a rapid change in Reid's mood when he began recounting the story he told police earlier about seeing a dark car in Mona's driveway. Sergeant Neil commented, "I formed the impression that he committed the crime from his gestures. He was crouched in his chair in a bent over fetal position, grasping both of his arms. He had his feet underneath his chair in a defensive position. There were outward signs of nervousness and he was stammering."

Reid interrupted his story to inform Sergeant Neill that his wife Viola was in hospital at St. John's awaiting an operation. The Sergeant allowed him to make a telephone call to her. He recalled, "Reid was visibly shaken when he spoke to her and said, 'Stick with me, I love you. Do you love me? I'm here with the police about Mona.' He began crying loudly and I took the telephone.

"A woman was hysterical and crying aloud," testified Sergeant Neil. He explained that he told her she would be contacted as to the results of the investigation and he then hung up the telephone.

The witness said that after a few minutes Reid settled down and the polygraph testing was resumed. Sergeant

Neill picked up a pen and drew a circle on a piece of paper. He showed the circle to Reid and commented, "You have told me part of the story, but it has not gone the full circle."

Neill began questioning Reid about his relationship with Rose. At this point, according to the witness, the accused became upset and showed signs of agitation. When Sergeant Neill suggested that Reid believed he was seeing Rose and not Mona Johnson, Reid exploded. He began crying and shouting, "It was Rose. It was Rose!" Neill described the physical effects of the suggestion on Reid: "Reid's body was shaking and he was stammering and crying aloud at that point."

Reid blurted out, "She was laughing at me. She had my baby in her arms and was jamming a plastic shoehorn down his throat. He was choking. I hit her! I hit her! She fell down and I set fire to the house and ran."

Sergeant Neill made no comment. He watched the accused's reaction and listened carefully to every word uttered. After a pause in telling his story Reid looked at the police sergeant and commented, "Oh my God! What's Viola going to think. I don't want to be locked up." Reid thought for a moment then added, "Rose looked like Mona. I hit her, she fell back."

Sergeant Neill sensed the inner torment and anguish building up inside Reid. He grabbed Reid's arm with one hand and with the other squeezed his hand. The sergeant recalled that at this point, "The blood drained from his face and he appeared to lose consciousness for several seconds. When he regained composure he was sweating profusely from his forehead." Sergeant Neill encouraged Reid to take a break and rest awhile. He helped the accused to a bed in the room.

Under cross-examination, the defence lawyer asked Sergeant Neill if Reid had mentioned at anytime having sex with the victim. Neill replied that he felt if the accused did have sex with the victim he would have found it disgusting because of his wife, and he would not have wanted to talk about it.

The court was distracted at this point by the actions of the accused in the witness box. Reid jumped to his feet and attempted to address Justice Mifflin. "My Lord, My Lord," he shouted. But Judge Mifflin sternly interrupted and ordered him to sit down. He told Reid that his lawyer would speak on his behalf. He then called a recess to allow the witness time to settle down.

When the trial resumed a witness who was with Reid on the night of February 3rd testified. Seymour Dalton told the court they were together drinking and shared three dozen beers with two other friends. After that, he said, they dropped Reid off on a road near the home of Mona Johnson. It was 12:40 a.m. He commented, "Andrew Reid was perfectly all right when dropped off." The prosecution called several witnesses who testified that they were in the area that night and did not see any car at Mona Johnson's.

Henrietta Reid who lived near Andrew Reid told the court that she saw the accused sometime after 4:40 a.m. on February 4. Mrs. Reid said she looked out her window and saw Andrew Reid running from his house with something in his left hand. He went into an outhouse, she testified. Police had determined that Reid dumped his clothing into the outhouse. When recovered they found blood stains on the items.

Evidence was presented to reinforce the prosecution's claim that the victim had been raped. Lucy Bishop, an expert from the RCMP Crime Laboratory at Sackville, New Brunswick testified that seminal fluid was found in specimens taken from Mrs. Johnson's vagina.

Mrs. Bishop also told the court that the blood stains found on a shirt and parka discarded by the accused in an outhouse were similar to Mona Johnson's blood type.

The police expert explained that both Andrew Reid and Mona Johnson had rare blood types. She noted that Mona Johnson's blood type is found, ". . . in only eight percent of the population. Eight in one thousand. Andrew Reid's blood type is found only in seven percent or seven in one thousand."

When cross-examined by the defence, the witness said that blood types are likely to be similar in small communities. Mrs. Bishop concluded her testimony by telling the court that, "No traces of alcohol were found in blood samples of the victim."

Another witness from the RCMP Crime Lab, Doug Shields, gave evidence regarding the wire used to strangle Mona Johnson. Mr. Shields, a chemistry expert, testified that careful analysis of the wire found around the victim's neck was similar to the wire found on a telephone in the Johnson home.

Another Crown witness and friend of Mona Johnson's, Levi Warren, was called to give evidence. Mr. Warren, from Bonavista, was a linesman with the Canadian National Telegraph Corporation. He told the court he had installed a telephone in the kitchen at Mona Johnson's house. He said the cord connecting the telephone to a connection box on the wall measured five and a half feet in length. This was the same length as the wire found tightly wrapped around the victim's neck.

With the case of the prosecution concluded the defence called the accused, Andrew Scott Reid, to the stand. Reid had completed high school at Little Catalina. He moved to St. John's to attend an accounting course at the College of Trades and Technology. He also completed several upgrading courses at the Canadian National School for the Blind at Halifax, Nova Scotia. (Reid had only ten percent of his vision due to impairment of his optic nerve.)

The usual shuffling, movement and whispering among spectators at a trial came to an abrupt stop when Reid began telling his side of the story as to what happened to Mona Johnson. Spectators were surprised to see the witness so calm and apparently in control as he gave evidence.

However, the trial became even more bizarre than before. Reid refuted the statements he gave to police and gave a drastically different account of events leading up to the killing of Mona Johnson.

He testified that two unknown assailants had overpowered him when he visited Mona Johnson on the night of the murder. He claimed they demanded his silence by threatening to kill his wife and child if he ever told authorities that they killed Mona Johnson and burned her house. This was in contradiction to his statement to the police that he murdered Mona Johnson because he believed she was an ex-fiancée.

The witness was composed and confident as he told the court that he and three friends were hanging out in a parked car the night of the murder. He explained they were drinking beer and singing songs. In addition to the beer, according to Reid, they also consumed three quarters of a flask of moonshine at his house when they went to pick up a guitar.

The accused told the court that his fourteen-month-old son was staying with his mother-in-law in Melrose, five miles from Little Catalina.

By 1:15 a.m., Reid said, they were ready to call it a night. He asked his friends to drop him off on the road near Mona Johnson's and suggested that from there he would hitchhike to Melrose to stay with his son.

The coldness of the winter night caused Reid to change his mind. When his friends dropped him off he waited awhile but there were no cars on the road. He recalled that the alcohol had taken its affect on him and he had problems walking. He decided to go to Mona Johnson's and telephone his brother for a drive home. The witness said that the victim was his cousin, but he had not seen her since December, 1974.

Reid testified that he walked to the back door of the Johnson house and noticed the outside door was slightly opened. He said, "I knocked. There was no answer. I walked in. The kitchen was dark. The next thing I knew

I was knocked to the floor by someone. I was pinned partially face down and I heard voices saying, 'Hurry up we got to get out of here. We got to get out of the province tonight'."

Reid continued, "Then a man with dark hair and wearing a brown leather jacket came on the scene. The man rushed into the bedroom while the other man had him pinned to the floor. He returned from the room with something in his hand. He pushed what seemed to be clothing in my face and there was something wet on it. The man holding me said 'Hurry light the fire.' When the other man went into the bedroom I saw the flickering light. The man set fire to the bed clothes. When he came out he said, 'Let's get out of here'."

The accused then alleged that he was threatened by the assailants. He recalled, "Before they left, one man grabbed me by the hair and hauled my head back. He told me the best thing for me to do was to get out of the house. He said, 'If you say anything you won't have a wife or kids for long'." Reid said the two men then fled through the kitchen door.

Meanwhile, according to Reid, he was trembling with fear and his arm was in agonizing pain. He said he got to his feet and went into the bedroom but the bed and wall were ablaze. He added, "There was a body on the floor but I couldn't tell who it was because it was face down."

He described his effort to help the woman. Reid said he placed his hands under her and tried to lift her. He claimed that as he did the woman fell against his chest and he saw blood . . . and something around her neck.

"I really got scared," Reid said. "I dropped the body and ran. I just ran until I got home."

When asked under cross-examination why he did not report this to someone immediately, he answered that the threatening words of the assailants kept coming into his head. Reid explained that when he arrived home he looked into the bathroom mirror and noticed he was covered in blood. He said, "There was blood on my face, on my jacket and shirt. I took off the jacket and shirt and I washed the blood off my face."

The accused said he went to bed, but he couldn't sleep. He was restless and tossing and turning. He couldn't get the murder scene off his mind. He got up out of bed and set out to hide his blood-stained clothing.

Reid recalled that when he heard two police officers talking to his grandmother about Mona's death on February 6 he decided to tell them what happened. However, his recollection of the warning and threats given by the killers caused him to change his mind and give a different story.

Reid said when the police first suggested that he submit to a polygraph test he agreed. However, after some careful thought he decided it would be better to refuse it. He finally agreed to the test however, because he felt that if he refused it would make the police even more suspicious of his role in the crime.

The witness recalled that his emotions began to build up inside him when the door to the polygraph room closed and he was left alone with Sergeant Neill and the lie-detector machine. He recalled that everything that happened was running through his mind and he was becoming tormented.

Reid said he became even more agitated when Sergeant Neill began asking personal questions. He said the story about Rose trying to kill his son originated with the police expert. He told the court he went along with the sergeant's suggestion that he killed Mona because he believed she was Rose, his ex-girl friend.

The witness explained that Sergeant Neill told him if that is what he thought happened, it would be manslaughter not murder. He added that he decided it would be better to go to jail for manslaughter than to have something happen to his son.

By the conclusion of the trial the prosecution had called thirty-seven witnesses while the defence called only one, Andrew Scott Reid.

In his summation to the jury, Robert Wells argued that the Crown had not proven its case. He suggested that the Crown's case was based on the theory that the accused visited Mrs. Johnson on February 4 for sex. However, the evidence had not clearly shown that the accused did have sex with the victim. Mr. Wells stressed that at no time in talking to police did the accused admit to having sex with the victim.

Prosecutor Barry Hill felt the evidence spoke strongly for the guilt of Andrew Reid. Mr. Hill argued that, "It's an insult to the intelligence of everyone here. Never before have you been subjected to such an arrogant story. Andrew Reid went to Mona Johnson's for sex and the sexual portion of the crime was too repulsive for him to admit."

In his address to the twelve member all-male jury, Judge Mifflin described the killing of Mona Johnson as, ". . . a horrible and horrendous crime." He flatly told the jury he did not believe the testimony of Andrew Reid. However, he explained, while it is not unusual for a trial judge to express his opinion on the evidence, "You the jury are in no way bound to abide by my opinion."

Judge Mifflin stated that Reid had tried to extricate himself from the crime by offering to assist the police in their investigation when they came to his home on the morning of February 6.

The judge described Andrew Reid as, ". . . a pretty sophisticated individual. At one point he thought he could even beat the polygraph test which the police had arranged for him to take."

Reid, he continued, was clever enough to know when he was trapped and he seized on the illusion of his ex-girl friend Rose when it was suggested by police. The Judge added, "He still thinks he can deceive you or me today. He's a rather imaginative person. His testimony is too ridiculous to talk about." Judge Mifflin concluded that there is no obligation on the Crown to show what prompts a person to commit an offence.

The jury convened on Friday, June 25 to consider the evidence and arrive at a verdict. Their work took only one hour and twenty minutes. Alex Miller, foreman of the jury announced the verdict of guilty as charged. The conviction carried a mandatory life sentence.

Judge Mifflin then advised the jury they could recommend a parole date if they chose. He explained that the convicted man must serve at least ten years before becoming eligible for parole. However, the jury could recommend anywhere between ten and twenty years. The jury chose not to make a recommendation, leaving that decision to the court.

The judge expressed his gratitude to the jury for their work and told them, "... it was the only decision you could come to."

Judge Mifflin then asked Reid to stand to be sentenced. Reid was in tears as the judge sentenced him to life imprisonment. His wife Viola also broke into tears and was escorted from the courtroom by friends. She had sat in the courtroom throughout the nine day trial.

As police officers escorted Reid from the courtroom he lost consciousness and stumbled. A short while later he was on his feet and led from the courtroom to begin serving his life sentence.

OLD TIME JUSTICE

ATTACKED WITH AN AXE

TO BE A POLICE OFFICER IN ST. JOHN'S during the early days of this century required courage and strength. There were no two-way radios to call for back-up when in danger, no guns in the trunk of a car — no car. Police officers of the era have been frequently described as tall, powerful and fearless men. One police officer who epitomized the characteristics needed to succeed in that profession was Constable Stapleton. Many stories were told of his heroics and his humorous contacts with some of the well known characters of the town. One such character was Mickey Quinn.

One story, which would have sent chills up the spine of even an armed policeman, was based on a true encounter between Stapleton and a madman on Military Road in 1906.

The Evening Telegram reported the incident on July 24, 1906 under the headline **Attacked With a Pick Axe**. It read:

> "Hugh Walsh, a labourer of the East End became insane on Rawlin's Cross yesterday afternoon and attacked Constable Stapleton with a pick axe. He made a blow at the officer's head, and

had it struck the intended place would undoubtedly have killed him instantly. It was an unpleasant moment for the officer, but there was nothing left for him to do but wrestle with his infuriated opponent. Walsh is a burly man, and one not easy overpowered.

"Fortunately for Stapleton, he succeeded in grasping the axe; he endeavoured to take it, but found it too heavy a task, as Walsh was bent on destruction and would not give it up. After some minutes of desperate struggling, the Constable, by Herculean strength, managed to tear it from the madman and fling it out of harms way. Walsh then fought with his fists, but being minus the pick axe the officer felt in better humour to contend with him.

"Walsh, however, was not to be easily overcome, and he worked like a demon. Stapleton's hope was to handcuff him, but this was more than he could do alone. He succeeded in throwing him to the ground and held him until Cornelius Pender and a couple of other civilians happened along to his assistance.

"Hughie struggled, but notwithstanding the bracelet's were adjusted, but a minute later he pulled his hands through. Similar trouble was experienced in putting them on the second time, but they completed the job, and calling a cab drove their man to the police station.

"Upon reaching the door Walsh showed fight once again, and two other officers were necessary to carry him into the station. He was laid on the floor, and kicked the men as they put on a strait jacket.

"Sgt. Corbett was on guard and barely escaped being bitten by the frenzied man. They also found it necessary to bind his feet before putting him in the cell. It was a sad sight to witness the unfortunate. Being unable to do the police hurt, he pounded his head on the floor with terrible force three or four times. His cries could be heard for blocks away. Dr. Rendell was summoned and after making an examination, pronounced him insane, and soon after he was driven to the asylum. It is well that Stapleton was the first person attacked or the results would have been terrible to contemplate.

"There were several children about, and how they escaped the eye of the lunatic is a mystery. Walsh has been at the Asylum several times before and on one or two occasions, when he felt himself becoming deranged, went to the lockup and gave himself in charge. Constable Stapleton is to be congratulated on his escape; had he been less courageous, perhaps, he would not be as sound in limb today."

During another, more amusing incident, Stapleton matched wits with the town character Mickey Quinn.

Quinn was resting in a boarding house on Williams Lane off Water Street when a friend rushed in to tell him that a large crate full of bologna had broken on the wharf. The friend told Mickey that Stapleton was standing guard over the scattered property until it could be accounted for and re-crated.

Quinn accepted a challenge and bet from others in the boarding home that he could not penetrate the security on the wharf to steal a bologna.

In minutes, Quinn was standing on the wharf sizing up the situation. Sure enough, the bologna was spread all over the place, but under the watchful eye of Constable Stapleton. Quinn eluded the policeman and got onto the wharf. However, when he attempted to leave the area with an obvious bulge sticking out from his overcoat, Stapleton stopped him and asked what he was hiding.

Quinn replied, "Nothing, only me pet cat. She ran down the wharf and I found her among the bologna."

Stapleton: "You think I was born yesterday Quinn? Open your coat!"

Quinn: "I'd rather not, sir, because she might get away."

Stapleton: "I insist. You open your coat right now or I'll take you to the lockup."

Quinn: "All right, sir." Just as he opened the coat, out jumped a big black tomcat and ran down the wharf. Stapleton, red faced, apologized to Quinn and told him to go find his cat.

Minutes later Quinn, again leaving the wharf with his coat bulging out, encountered Stapleton. This time Stapleton commented, "I see you found your cat, Mickey." To which Quinn replied, "Thank the lord," and continued to walk up the street.

When he entered the boarding house he shouted to his friends, "Well I done it, I got the bologna, now pay up." Opening his coat he pulled out a full bologna. But Quinn was surprised at the lack of enthusiasm showed by his buddies.

Then he heard a loud meow. When he turned he saw that the black cat had followed him, and Corporal Stapleton had followed the black cat. The police officer recovered the stolen bologna and Mickey found himself cooling off in the lockup.

THE BRAWL ON McNEIL STREET

During the first decade of this century police were often called to the Rabbit Town area to break up brawling. The following item which appeared in *The Daily News* during July, 1910 gives a glimpse of the neighbourhood at that time. The headline read **"The Police Stop A Love Feast."**

"McNeil Street, otherwise known as 'Rabbit Town' and famous for neighbourly love feasts was the centre of police attraction last night. Another such entertainment was in full swing from 7:30 to 9:00 o'clock, when the curtain rang down with a grand tableau showing Constables O'Keefe and Lawlor arresting the entertainer-in-chief and about a score of militant Amazons attempting to rescue the prisoner.

"The quiet of the evening had been disturbed by one of the women residents of the street saying unkind things of her neighbour's husband, and within a few minutes the disturbance was general. Men mixed it up lively with fisticuffs while women engaged in the milder form of removing each others hair by the painless system of 'pulling.'

"Supt. Grimes, Constables Stamp, Lawlor and O'Keefe, were hurriedly ordered to the front, but the belligerents occupied a fortified position and were fighting in their own territory and H.M. forces were obliged to retreat.

"A strategical movement on the part of the Supt., however, made the enemy abandon their positions, and in their eagerness to withdraw to a place of safety, left their leader on the field, who was taken prisoner. He fought to the last, when surrounded, and when the steel bands were placed on him, his regimentals were reduced to the minimum.

"The police made two other visits during the night, but the sentries gave the alarm each time and no further prisoners were taken. The one and only will appear this morning and it is likely many of those taking part in the disturbance will be summoned for disorderly conduct."

The culprits were given $2.00 fines by the magistrate and a stiff dressing down. It was some time before police had to be called again to McNeil Street.

A SMART LAWYER?

During the summer of 1912 a man was being tried in court at Ferryland for stealing a neighbour's farm equipment. The accused pleaded not guilty and hired a "...smart, gentleman lawyer from the City." (St. John's).

The complainant, a farmer named Cahill, had just been questioned by the prosecutor. The city lawyer smiled and leaning towards his client whispered, ". . . no problem here."

The defence lawyer began his strategic attack. "You say, that you can swear to having seen this man drive a horse past your farm on the day in question?"

"I can," replied Cahill wearily, for he had already answered the question a dozen times for the prosecutor.

"What time was that?" queried the defence.

Cahill answered, "I told you it was about the middle of the forenoon."

"But I don't want any 'abouts' or any 'middles'! I want you to tell the jury exactly the time."

"Why?" said Cahill. "I don't always carry a gold watch with me when I am digging potatoes."

"But you have a clock in the house haven't you?" retorted the lawyer.

"Yes," answered the witness.

"Well, what time was it by that?" asked the lawyer.

"Well, by that clock it was just nineteen minutes past ten,"said Cahill.

"You were in the field all that morning?" went on the lawyer smiling suggestively.

"I was," said Cahill.

"How far from the house is the field?" the lawyer asked.

Cahill replied, "About half a mile."

"You swear, do you, that by the clock in your house it was exactly nineteen minutes past ten?"

"I do," answered Cahill.

The lawyer paused and looked triumphantly at the jury. At last he had entrapped the old farmer into a statement that would greatly weaken his evidence.

"I think that will do," said the lawyer, with a wave of his hand. "I have quite finished with you."

Cahill leisurely picked up his hat and started to leave the witness box.

"I ought perhaps to say, yer honour," he added, "that too much reliance should not be placed on that clock as it got out of gear about six months ago, and it's been nineteen minutes past ten ever since."

Old timers say that lawyer never showed his face around the Shore again.

THE WHEEL OF FORTUNE SPINS

A CARNIVAL ATMOSPHERE prevailed throughout the city of St. John's on Thursday, August 8, 1968. It was Regatta Day, a civic holiday. The city seemed deserted. More than 20,000 citizens went to Quidi Vidi Lake in the City's east end. Thousands of others enjoyed the holiday by going to the country. Among the crowd at Quidi Vidi was thirty-three-year-old Gerard Parsons.

Parsons plodded his way through the shoulder-to-shoulder crowd which gathered to enjoy the day at the races. Occasionally he stopped near a concession tent scanning the crowd for a familiar face or to try his luck at a wheel of fortune. He got lucky at a goods wheel after buying three tickets for a quarter. He was delighted when a number he was holding came up on the wheel. Scanning the array of prizes available to him, his eyes settled on a hunting knife. Pointing to it he shouted to be heard above the din of the crowd, "I'll take the knife."

Five hours later Parsons, in a fit of rage, was using the knife to savagely butcher the girl he had hoped to marry. By the time his rage spent itself, Audrey Ballett huddled dead in a pool of blood at the Parson's home on Prince of Wales Street.

What happened to trigger this anomalous behaviour from a usually quiet and well-behaved man may never be known. Only two people were in the house at the time of the murder. One of them was now dead. The other was facing a charge of non capital murder in the Supreme Court of Newfoundland.

The relationship between Parsons and Audrey Ballett, a native of Port Rexton, began on Easter Sunday in 1965. A friend had arranged for the two to meet on a blind date. The relationship blossomed and Parsons developed an obsession for the attractive and affable girl. He was proud and delighted in 1967 when she performed in the locally produced musical, Oliver.

Parsons had thoughts of marriage but he felt he was not financially secure enough to take on that responsibility. Soon after the musical performance Audrey decided to move to Toronto where she found work. Parsons was tormented and depressed over the separation. He saved his money and went to Toronto in October to visit her. Before he returned home, Audrey promised him she would come back to visit for her holidays in August. She told him she would go back to Toronto after her holidays. However, she would return to Nfld. for good in November, 1968. Audrey didn't like the idea of Parsons' drinking and she had no appreciation of Parsons' troubled personality. With Ballett gone, Parsons sank into a depression and began abusing alcohol. He had experienced problems with alcohol for fifteen years. These problems had intensified over recent years.

The combination of depression and alcohol abuse led to several suicide attempts and a series of stays on psychiatric wards of city hospitals. In 1959 and 1960 he was admitted to the Hospital for Mental and Nervous Diseases for treatment of alcohol abuse and depression.

Two months before Ballett returned to Newfoundland in August, 1968 he experienced a series of blackouts. He was deeply depressed and attempted suicide. Parsons wanted help. He signed himself into the Hospital for Mental and Nervous Diseases for treatment. By that time he was not eating and he had lost forty-five pounds. His stay at the hospital was short. In less than two days he signed himself out and again took up drinking.

Although Parsons knew he had problems and desperately wanted to be cured, he lacked the self-discipline to see himself succeed. When he began seeing things, he sank into another depression and again sought medical help. This time two doctors certified him for admission to the psychiatric ward at the Grace General Hospital.

The treatment was unsuccessful. Soon after his release he returned to the bottle. He felt so tormented that he again tried suicide. This attempt resulted in him being sent back to the Hospital for Mental and Nervous Diseases. When released from hospital, the doctors prescribed a supply of librium which he was instructed to take eight times a day. Among other things, Librium is used for the treatment of anxiety.

The drug therapy wasn't helping Parsons. His depression continued and he didn't know why. He returned to work at CN but had great difficulty concentrating. He displayed symptoms of manic depression, and experienced alternating periods of acute depression and elation. Since Parsons was finding it nearly impossible to concentrate, his employer switched him to less demanding work to accomodate him.

The weekend before the tragic killing of Ballett, Parsons was so depressed that he took a knife and tried to commit suicide. He was stopped through the physical intervention of his mother and brother.

On August 8, Regatta Day, 1968 Parsons was required to work. He had been drinking the night before and in the morning was experiencing a hangover. He hadn't eaten in days. That morning he passed up breakfast and took two libriums before leaving for work. The last thing on his mind that day was murder. The last thing on Audrey Ballett's mind was becoming a murder victim.

Audrey had arrived back in St. John's to spend her summer holidays. She was joyful and looking forward to seeing old friends. She called the Parsons household and left a message with Mary Parsons, Gerard's mother, to tell him she was back in town.

When Parsons arrived home for dinner at 12:30 p.m. his mother told him the good news. Suddenly his depression changed to joy. His mother told him, "Audrey called for you this morning. She's back in town." Gerard couldn't wait for her to call back. He tracked her down by telephone and expressed a wish to see her.

While Parsons was jubilant in anticipation of seeing Audrey, it seemed Audrey was less enthusiastic. She had decided to go to the Regatta with friends that afternoon but promised Gerard that she would meet him at his house at around 6:15 p.m.

Parsons was obsessed with seeing Audrey. Returning to work that afternoon was out of the question, so he called in sick, and took the afternoon off. He popped two more libriums and decided to go down to the Regatta. Perhaps he might run into Audrey at lakeside.

On his way to Quidi Vidi he stopped for two beers at Hotel Newfoundland. At Quidi Vidi he spent two hours browsing through the crowds. He stopped at a wheel of fortune and won a hunter's knife. Parsons continued looking around for a familiar face, but there was no sign of Audrey. At around 4:30 he went back to Hotel Newfoundland and consumed two more beers. At the hotel he showed off his knife and tried to sell it. He asked several patrons if they knew how much the knife was worth.

At 5:30 p.m. he got a taxi and went home, still in possession of the hunting knife. He went to the kitchen and put the knife away.

There was little doubt that Parsons was eagerly anticipating his meeting with Audrey Ballett. However, Audrey appeared more restrained. At 6:00 p.m. she called Parsons to explain that she would not be dropping over to his house as planned at 6:15. The girl noted that she decided instead to accompany friend Margaret Ploughman to visit a friend at the Grace General Hospital. She promised to visit him right after the hospital visit.

Parsons again became anxious and instead of waiting walked over to the Grace to visit a friend, and hopefully to run into his girl friend. The friend had been released earlier that day but the visit was not in vain. While in the lobby he finally came face to face with Audrey and he was elated.

Margaret recalled that Parsons had been drinking. She said, "There was a smell of liquor on his breath but he wasn't intoxicated." Commenting on Parsons behaviour, Margaret said, "He seemed quite excited and he was talking rapidly, saying it was a long time since he had seen Audrey." Audrey told Parsons to go to his house and she would visit him at 8:15 p.m. He agreed and left the hospital.

When she failed to turn up at 8:15, Parsons left his house and met the two girls at the intersection of Gear Street and Prince of Wales Street. The trio returned to his home. Audrey gave Parsons a new shirt and gave his mother an ornament.

Mary Parsons and Margaret Ploughman left the house to visit friends and to give Gerard and Audrey a chance to spend some time alone. Mary Parsons visited a neighbour, Mrs. Gertrude Fleming, while Margaret went to the home of a friend on Franklyn Avenue.

Margaret called Audrey at 9:30 and everything seemed fine. When she called again at 11:15, a policeman answered.

Mary Parsons had returned home at 11:00 and found the doors locked and the lights out. Through a slot in a Venetian blind in the living room window she could see Audrey partly on the chesterfield. She sensed something was wrong. But, she didn't know if the girl was dead.

Mrs. Parsons sought the help of her friend Mrs. Fleming and they entered the home through a rear door. Mrs. Parsons switched on the lights in the kitchen and hallway. The living room was still in darkness. She walked to the living room door. By the light shining through the window she could see the blood covered body of Audrey Ballett.

Stunned by the shocking sight, Mary Parsons shook the body crying out "Audrey, Audrey!"

The realization that something terrible had happened sent Mrs. Parsons running back to the kitchen to tell her friend, "My God she's got her throat cut." The two women went to Fleming's and called the police.

One of the first constabulary officers to arrive at the scene was Detective Eric Penney. Penney was nearing the end of his shift and driving fellow detective Len Simms home when he was directed by the dispatcher at police headquarters to proceed directly to 38 Prince of Wales Street. There was no indication of what had taken place. But the police officers knew it was something serious. Their expectations were confirmed as they entered the house. There was blood on the walls inside and out; the interior indicated a struggle had taken place and in the living room the young police officer was horrified to see the blood-covered body of a young woman.

While the police were converging on 38 Prince of Wales Street, Parsons was making a getaway in a taxi operated by Ted Hollohan.

Parsons, originally had gotten into a taxi operated by Hollohan's father. However, the driver did not want to go to Flatrock so he stopped by the Waldegrave Street stand where Ted worked and offered the fare to him. Ted agreed and Parsons transferred to the second cab.

It was about 10:30 when Parsons entered Hollohan's taxi. Ted recalled, "I didn't know it was Parsons. On the way to Flatrock we chatted about the weather and the Regatta." Ted saw nothing unusual in the behaviour of Gerard Parsons. He commented, "Parsons didn't appear to be drinking though it was possible he could have." They stopped at a tavern so Parsons could pick up some beer then went on to Flatrock.

"When he got out," explained Hollohan, "I noticed blood on his pant leg. I wasn't suspicious when I saw the blood. He could have been drinking and in a fight; he could have cut himself . . . there could have been any number of reasons why he had blood on his pants."

Ted Hollohan described Parson's mood: "He wasn't nervous . . . as a matter of fact he was as cool and calm as a person who had just returned from a trip to Florida. I heard Parsons wiping his hands on the back seat. He said his hands were sticky from eating chicken and chips. I had no reason to suspect anything was wrong."

Parsons spent about five minutes at his dad's house. He told Hollohan that he was trying to borrow his brother's car. He then asked Hollohan to drive him to a girl friend's house. Parsons'paid his fare and Hollohan returned to St. John's.

Meanwhile, Sergeant Don Randell was supervising police at the crime scene. He saw Audrey in a pool of blood on the floor of the living room. Her head was resting on a chesterfield cushion. One of her legs was on the coffee table, the other beneath it. Constable Ed Mercer picked up her arm to feel the pulse. There was none. Nor was there any other sign of life.

A quick look around the inside and outside of the house revealed to police that the victim had put up quite a struggle. Evidence indicated Audrey was attacked with the knife while on the outside steps and dragged back into the hallway and then the living room. More than sixty-four knife wounds were inflicted upon the defenceless young woman.

Sim Wentzell, an identification expert with the police, began gathering the physical evidence for the trial he knew most certainly would follow.

Ted Hollohan had not seen the last of Gerard Parsons when he left him at Flatrock. Sergeant Randell was about three hours behind Parsons. The police had been visiting taxi stands around the city to find out if Parsons had taken a cab after the murder. About 2:00 a.m. they walked into the Waldegrave Street stand where Ted Hollohan was working. Their efforts paid off. Hollohan confirmed that he had driven a man fitting Parsons description to Flatrock earlier that night. Hollohan recalled, "I didn't notice anything up to that time." The police searched Hollohan's cab and found blood stains on the seat.

By daybreak Friday squads of police moved into the Flatrock area. They set up roadblocks in the north east area of St. John's and obtained the services of an RCMP police dog. A police guard was posted outside the Parsons home on Prince of Wales Street.

Rumours that a murder had occurred spread rapidly around St. John's. In the early stages very little information was available. On Friday, August 9, Head Constable Nick Shannahan got an arrest warrant from Magistrate Hugh O'Neill for thirty-three-year-old Gerard Parsons. By Sunday the press had confirmed a murder had taken place and a manhunt was underway. This created problems for the police who had to contend with traffic jams caused by curious motorists. The police were stopping and searching all cars entering and leaving the Flatrock area.

Police were certain Parsons was still in the area. He was born there, knew the area well and could hide out for weeks. Randell had investigated and learned that there had been no boats or cars stolen. He noted there were many small shacks and vegetable cellars in the area where a person could hide. Also, Parsons could survive on berries, vegetables and fish, which were plentiful. By Monday police released an accurate artist's sketch of Parsons. He was 5 ft. 9 in. tall, weighed 140 pounds and had black bushy hair. He was wearing light green pants, a light green sports jacket, a green shirt and tan and dark shoes. There were blood stains on the pants. The publicity resulted in hundreds of reports of sightings of the fugitive. Every available Constabulary officer was involved in the manhunt.

Parsons eluded police for five days before a combined search party made up of Constabulary and RCMP officers tracked him down.

On Monday, August 12, at 10:20 a.m. the fugitive was apprehended by RCMP Constable Everett Carrol, wearing the same clothes he wore on the night of the crime. Parsons did not resist arrest. While being searched he asked Carrol to button his coat. Referring to the blood stains on his shirt he commented, "Button it up. I don't want to look at it. The police reported that Parsons had not been given aid by anyone. He looked tired and hungry. Police searched the area for evidence, then brought their man to police headquarters at Fort Townshend where he was photographed and fingerprinted. Radio news bulletins then informed the public of the arrest. The reports noted that Parsons was to be arraigned in court that day.

Public interest in the case was similar to the type shown in the earlier part of this century when crowds surrounded the court house during criminal trials. Crowds gathered outside the court house on this August day and waited five hours to get a glimpse of the accused. Well-known Telegram reporter Jim Stratton wrote, "Nobody would leave the line-up. They sent kids for Pepsi and chips. They wouldn't risk leaving, afraid they might lose their vantage point."

Police were kept busy trying to control the crowds and keep the kids off the walls, steps and driveway. Stratton noted, "On more than one occasion kids and adults came close to injury when they struggled ahead each time a police vehicle arrived."

One police officer commented, "Stupid! Don't they know it's a sick man they're bringing here, not a freak?"

When the police car arrived, Parsons was escorted into court by Head Constable Shannahan. The crowd did not show any sentiment. They had waited five hours out of curiosity just to get a look at the man to be charged with murder.

The Evening Telegram was highly critical of the Royal Newfoundland Constabulary for not cooperating with the media during the early hours of the manhunt. On Tuesday, August 13, the day after Parsons was captured, the

Telegram published an editorial critical of the police. It was entitled, "Police Caught in Own Web."

The editorial stated: "The actions of the St. John's police, probably only laughable in simple matters like parking tickets, can be highly dangerous when a serious crime is committed. The murder of a young woman on Thursday night is a case in point."

The editorial expressed the opinion that the police should have confirmed the obvious. It said, "From the description of the wounds and the brutal treatment of the woman's body it would be obvious to the most junior policeman that the crime was murder. Yet the police refused to confirm that any crime had been committed at all until late on Friday morning."

The paper suggested that police handling of the manhunt was instrumental in the fugitive eluding police for five days. It noted, "From the moment the body was discovered somewhere between 9:30 and 11:30 on Thursday night until 1:30 on Friday morning it was as if every action of the police was designed to give the wanted person more time to escape or to commit another crime. The police refused to confirm that a person was being sought, refused to give a description of the person and behaved generally as if the news media were interfering in the pursuit of justice by asking questions."

The editorial criticized the police for failing to warn the public. It stated, ". . . no description of the man was released until more than 12 hours after the crime was committed, although they must have been aware of the identity of the person they were seeking within minutes of discovering the body."

The editorial continued, "The obvious step would have been to broadcast a description of the man on the early morning news broadcasts and to publish his description and pictures in both daily newspapers on Friday." It added that ". . . if the full description of the wanted man had been given out (as it could have been) in the early hours of Friday morning, he might well have been in custody within hours of its publication.

The most scathing criticism levelled by the editorial stated, "The minister of justice can hardly be blamed for inheriting such a police force but he can be faulted for not having done something about it in the time he has been in office."

After Parsons was charged in court, the judge ordered him sent to the Mental Hospital for psychiatric evaluation. Testing at the hospital determined the accused was fit to stand trial.

The preliminary hearing got underway on October 11, and twenty-one witnesses were called. During this era Newfoundland had the Grand Jury system. Instead of being committed to stand trial, the preliminary inquiry sent the case to the Grand Jury.

The Grand Jury reviewed the evidence given at the preliminary and made a decision on whether there was enough evidence to go to trial. They returned, ". . . a full bill of indictment against Parsons."

The trial got underway on November 18 in Supreme Court before Justice R.S. Furlong. Parsons was represented by Robert Wells, and James Power, director of public prosecutions, represented the Crown. The twelve jury members were: Cyril O'Neill, Ira Bailey, John Cooper, Emmanual Billard, Leo King, Frank Mullett, Harry Curtis, Walter Pottle, Harris Clarke, Victor Batstone, Clement Dunphy and Douglas Kearsey.

Evidence presented by the Crown showed that a violent struggle had taken place with the victim trying to get away from her attacker. Sergeant Don Randell gave graphic evidence describing the bloody murder scene.

He testified, "There were blood stains on the lock of the front door, on the railing leading to the verandah of the house, on the house itself. There were also some blood stains on the adjoining house, number 38A." The police sergeant told the court the knife attack started on the verandah. He said, "I concluded she was stabbed on the verandah of the house and dragged inside. During the struggle they knocked the hall stove out of position. She held onto the door jamb and tried not to be dragged into the living room."

When Sergeant Randell entered the house he examined the living room where the body was found. He told the court, "All the blinds were closed. On the chesterfield was an empty sheath-knife case. On the floor I found two letters addressed to Parsons and signed by Audrey Ballett."

Evidence of the struggle inside the house was given by Randell. He testified, "The heavy oil stove in the hall was shifted about two inches. The stove pipes were disarranged and hanging on the stairs leading to the second story.

"The light switch in the hallway near the living room had stains of blood on it. The door jamb leading to the living room was also smeared in blood."

Sergeant Randell was present at the autopsy and he told the court he counted sixty-four stab wounds on the body of the victim. There were fourteen cuts and stab wounds on her right arm and hand. This showed the deceased may have been defending herself. He told the court that he examined the clothes worn by Parsons when arrested and found the shirt and pants stained with blood.

While hiding out in the woods Parsons penned a note on two blank cheques. The note indicated that he was not aware that Audrey was dead. The note read, "It was not her fault. It was mine and drinking. She wanted to get married three years ago and go to Toronto. I hope she is not dead or hurt. I do not remember all that happened or why. All my property I have I want left to my mother. I am mentally sick and now am sicker." The note was signed by Gerard Parsons.

Constable Simeon Wentzell was sent to the murder scene minutes after the police learned of the crime. His evidence also showed a struggle and brutal killing. He testified that he arrived at the murder scene at 11:15 p.m. He said he saw knife wounds on the victim's neck, face, arms and head. "There was blood on the floor near where she was sitting. Her clothes had bloodstains on them and the chesterfield was saturated with blood," Wentzell told the court. The witness added that he also found a towel in the bathroom with bloodstains on it.

Throughout the trial Parsons sat in the prisoner's box guarded by two policemen wearing piked helmets and dark suits. He stared straight ahead as though unaware of what was going on around him. Occasionally he bowed his head slightly and closed his eyes from time to time as evidence was being presented.

Two police officers gave testimony that on separate occasions the accused had told them that he had stabbed the victim.

Constable William Taylor interviewed the accused in an RCMP car at Shoe Cove shortly after his capture. Taylor was alone in the car with Parsons. The RCMP officers were standing nearby outside. The police witness told the court that he gave the customary caution to Parsons after which Parsons asked, "Is she dead?"

Taylor added that Parsons told him, ". . . I stabbed her once. I think some more, but I don't remember too well. I found the knife in my pocket and threw it down in the water near where I was picked up."

At this point, defence lawyer Wells objected to the admissibility of the evidence. He argued that the accused had spent five days in the open and was in no position to understand the police caution.

Judge Furlong directed the jury to leave and he conducted a Voir Dire (trial within a trial). Wells put Parsons on the witness stand and asked him if he was cautioned by Constable Taylor.

Parsons replied, "I don't remember any caution from Constable Taylor." He did, however, recall being asked why he did it.

Mr. Wells asked Parsons, "Did you understand that you did not have to speak if you didn't want to?"

The accused answered, "I was not aware of it. Although I did become aware of it later."

The Crown prosecutor asked him if he was aware through reading or conversation about a police caution. He replied, "I was not."

Judge Furlong ruled the evidence admissible and the jury were recalled into the court room where the trial continued.

Constable Art Pike also testified that Parsons admitted to him that he stabbed Audrey Ballett. Pike said that Parsons told him that he and the victim argued at his house and he stabbed her three or four times in the stomach. The accused said she was breathing hard and he was going to call an ambulance but was frightened.

The police officer told the court that Parsons said he felt his mother would soon be home and expected she would call an ambulance. Pike noted, "He said when he left the house the girl was breathing heavily on the chesterfield."

The next Crown witness was Hedley Preston, a bartender at Hotel Newfoundland. He described Parsons' visits to the bar on the afternoon of the murder. He told of Parsons drinking beer and showing his knife to other patrons of the bar. Preston said he was trying to sell it. Preston did not know how much liquor Parsons had consumed.

Taxi-driver John Payne took Parsons from the Hotel to his home on Prince of Wales Street the afternoon of the murder. He told the court that Parsons told him he had won the knife at the Regatta and wondered how much he would get for it. Payne said, "Parsons seemed to have a few drinks in, but apart from that his behaviour seemed normal."

The death certificate for Audrey Ballett was issued by pathologist Dr. Young Rho. Dr. Rho testified that during the autopsy he counted sixty-four stab wounds in the victim's body. He said, "These were found in the neck, chest, abdomen, thighs, hands and arms. The chest wound penetrated the heart, and the abdomen wounds had penetrated the stomach and liver."

Dr. Rho described how the girl died. He testified, "The fatal wounds were the one on the chest wall which penetrated the heart and the ones which penetrated the stomach and liver." He explained that the arm and hand wounds resulted from the deceased trying to defend herself.

Mr. Wells asked Dr. Rho, "Were these wounds caused by any great amount of force?"

Dr. Rho replied, "Sufficient strength to penetrate the skin and muscles."

The pathologist added that the wounds on the neck and the other minor wounds were inflicted after the fatal wounds were administered.

Throughout Dr. Rho's testimony there was a notable silence among spectators in the court room. Many sat on the edge of their seats and listened intently as the evidence unfolded. Occasionally, spectators exchanged glances and shook their heads.

During the testimony given by Dr. Rho a spectator collapsed and had to be carried from the court room.

Carol Kranack, an RCMP forensic expert, had examined the blood-stained evidence taken from the murder scene. However, the evidence disclosed little of value to the prosecution. She told the court that ". . . the blood on Parsons' clothing couldn't be identified because it was contaminated. However, some of the blood on the victim's clothing could be identified as group AM."

The blood-stained wood samples taken from the house also showed little. Kranack pointed out, ". . . there was insufficient quantity of blood present, to say if there were blood smears present or not. However, there was one scraping that had an indefinite human blood type." The witness could not determine the age of the blood scrapings.

The last Crown witness was Head Constable Nick Shannahan, who read the statement taken from Parsons on the day of his arrest. Shannahan told the court that Parsons was cautioned before he gave his statement.

In the statement Parsons recounted his activities throughout the day of August 8 to and following the murder. Shannahan testified that while Parsons and Ballett were alone she had asked him how much money he had. He told her, "Fourteen hundred dollars." Audrey told him that he had more money last year. To that Parsons replied, "I spent most of that in going up to see you last October."

Following this, according to Shannahan, Parsons went to his mother's room and found two bottles of beer and a bottle of whiskey. He drank the beer and took two drinks from the bottle of whiskey. He then went back to the living room and lay on the chesterfield with Audrey. Parsons told Shannahan that an argument erupted but he forgot what happened after that. Shannahan said Parsons remembered fighting with the victim. He didn't know why. The accused recalled wrestling with her, said Shannahan, but didn't remember stabbing her. The prosecution rested its case after Shannahan's testimony.

First witness for the defence was Gerard Parsons. The accused testified that on the day of the murder he had been drinking and taking librium. He said that at 8:00 p.m. he drank some after-shave lotion to take away the smell of liquor from his breath. Audrey Ballett did not approve of Gerard's drinking.

Parsons testified that, "When Audrey didn't show up by 8:15 as promised, I got depressed. I can't describe the feeling I had." The accused thought that she was not coming to his house. He decided to go to a downtown bar to get a few drinks. At the intersection of Gear Street and Prince of Wales Street he met Audrey and her friend Mary Ploughman. "We went to my house. I was overjoyed when I met her," Parsons told the court.

The accused's testimony now turned to the period

leading to the murder. In court, there was an obvious change in his presentation of evidence. His voice became high pitched and he began to stammer as he told the court of the last minutes of Audrey Ballett's life.

He said that his mother and Ploughman left them alone at his house. He said, "I remember Audrey asking me how much money I had saved up and I told her thirteen or fourteen hundred dollars, which was a lie. She told me I had more than that last year when she left to go to Toronto. I told her I got expenses to meet, such as a retirement insurance plan which she had asked me to take out."

Parsons continued, "She told me I had no money because I spent it on alcohol. We were lying on the chesterfield when the telephone rang. It was Mary Ploughman. I passed the phone to Audrey."

The evidence showed that by this time Parsons was working into a fury. When the telephone conversation ended he and Audrey argued over money and the possibility of buying a house. "I told her I had no money," he said. "I'm not sure if she was lying down or sitting up. She said she knew I was in hospital for drinking and told me I was lower than a snake. She said if I didn't stop drinking liquor once and for all she wouldn't see me again."

The argument upset Parsons. He told the court, "I called her some things, like double crosser and I said she was taking advantage of me. She looked like she was going to spit on me. I don't remember after that."

The accused testified that his next recollection was of Audrey sitting on the chesterfield with her feet on the floor and blood on her dress. He explained, "She was breathing hard and I went over and put my arms around her and I called her name. She didn't move."

Parsons panicked. First, he tried to call an ambulance. He dialled the telephone but he forgot what happened after that. He added, "I left the house. The next thing I remember is getting out of the taxi at Flatrock."

Wells asked Parsons to describe his feelings at that

time. He answered, "I don't know. I didn't have any feelings, because everything was blank — a daze — and I was in a state of shock."

He described hiding out in the woods near Shoe Cove. He recalled, "When I went into the woods I lay down. Two or three days later I noticed blood on the knife and I tossed it away. I was wet and tired but I didn't feel hungry." The accused added that he wrote a note telling what he had done because he was afraid he would die of hunger or be shot by police.

When asked by Wells if he remembered what happened he answered, "I have no memory of killing or stabbing the girl with the knife. I don't remember how I got the knife in my hands."

"What are your feelings towards Audrey Ballett?" asked Wells.

"I would sooner be dead than here now. When I killed her I killed myself," Gerard Parsons replied.

While being cross-examined the accused was asked, "Do you recall telling Constable Pike on the morning you were captured that you stabbed Audrey Ballett in the stomach?"

Parsons answered, "I remember talking to the police but I don't remember telling him that."

Power asked, "Why did you leave her in a bleeding condition?"

The accused replied, "I didn't know she was dying. At the present time I think it was a cruel and callous thing to do. I'm not capable of doing it now and wasn't capable before. It's a mystery to me, the same as it is to everyone else."

The defence attempted to show the jury that Parsons' use of alcohol and drugs had contributed to his brutal action. The defence called to the stand the superintendent at the Hospital for Mental and Nervous Diseases, Dr. J. Frazer Walsh.

Dr. Walsh described the drug librium and why it is prescribed. He testified, "Librium is used to treat alcoholics. The drug is a minor tranquilizer and is used to relieve tension and anxiety. It allows a person suffering from alcoholism to carry on without undue panic."

Dr. Walsh explained, "In extreme cases of alcoholism a dosage of up to 200 mgs. per day could be prescribed. When abused by taking with alcohol, or abused beyond prescribed dosages, trouble begins. Anyone combining the drug librium and alcohol over a long period of time could expect anything to happen."

In cross-examination Power asked Dr. Walsh to explain the effect that abuse could have on memory?

Dr. Walsh: "There has to be a mental explosion; if he cracked he wouldn't be able to act rationally and would over react to the situation. He wouldn't be able to control himself. A person may be able to recall some things but wouldn't know exactly what he did." Dr. Walsh noted that all his comments had to be applied to each particular person in each particular case.

Power interjected, "This is a situation in which a man had stabbed someone sixty-four times and says he could not remember. Is this the effect of the drug and alcohol or was it the accused just saying he couldn't remember?"

"It could be either," answered Dr. Walsh. He added, "A person taking Librium and alcohol may react in the opposite way to a situation. Instead of calming down he could become excited and act in an irrational manner."

A second psychiatric expert also testified. Dr. Francis Gillespie, Chief of Medical Services at the Hospital for Mental and Nervous Diseases, had interviewed Parsons during his assessment after the murder.

He described Parsons: "He has a personality disorder and it has been ingrained in him for a long time." He continued, "Parsons suffered from alcoholism and is immature with a life long tendency to become frustrated and impulsive. Parsons is psychopathic in that he didn't learn from the past." The doctor noted that Parsons had been treated a number of times for alcoholism.

Power asked, "If Parsons, because he had been drinking excessively and taking the drug, would he know what he was doing?"

Dr. Gillespie responded, "He would, up to a point. There is a cut off point before he would fall asleep and this is a shaded area."

Power: "Would stabbing Audrey Ballett be beyond Parsons control?"

Dr. Gillespie: "Maybe he didn't know what he was doing. Maybe he did."

Judge Furlong had a final question for the medical expert. The judge wondered if Parsons was treated for alcoholism and reverted to his ways upon release and did the same things again, "Was it not possible he could have committed a murder before under the right conditions?"

"There is no way of knowing," concluded Dr. Gillespie.

With the presentation of evidence completed. The court proceeded with the final summations by defence and prosecution.

Robert Wells argued that Parsons, on the day of the murder, was irrational and not aware of what he had done. He suggested that his client was guilty of manslaughter not capital murder.

Wells told the jury, "By having blackouts, by being an alcoholic, by taking librium and alcohol Parsons was not a rational person. His behaviour was irrational on the day of August 8." He stressed that the taking of librium, the consumption of alcohol, was such that Parsons could not control himself.

Wells said, "It was an indication of the state of mind Parsons was in, that when Audrey Ballett did not show up at his home at 8:15 as promised, Parsons could not control himself and he had to go out."

The defence lawyer asked, "Parsons had been despondent and elated all day. Why could Parsons consciously kill the girl he loved?"

Wells asked the jury to consider the evidence and bring in a verdict, ". . . not guilty of capital murder — but guilty of manslaughter."

James Carter argued to convict Gerard Parsons of non capital murder. Addressing the jury he said, "Parsons' behaviour before August 8 makes no difference. All that matters are the things he did on the evening of August 8."

Power continued, "Two people were left alone in a room and the events that happened covered a short period of time. Parsons had to leave the living room to go to the kitchen and get the knife. While Parsons' memory is very vague on the events of the death, he is very clear on what happened before and after."

Power added, "There was more deliberation than the accused admits. The taxi drivers who had driven Parsons to his home and to Flatrock considered he was acting normally.

"Mrs. Ploughman who met him at the hospital testified that although she smelt alcohol on his breath, she considered him to be normal. Parsons' story of not remembering events was completely self serving."

The prosecutor concluded, "It was not alcohol that killed Audrey Ballett. It was Gerard Parsons."

It was now the turn of Judge Furlong to deliver his direction to the jury. He cautioned, "A great responsibility rests on your shoulders. The Crown had to prove beyond a reasonable doubt that Parsons intended to kill the girl. The jury has to be satisfied that Parsons either didn't know what he was doing or didn't know that what he was doing was wrong."

After reviewing the evidence he told the jury, "You have the following options. First, to find him guilty of non capital murder. Second, not guilty of non capital murder. Third, not guilty by reason of insanity. Fourth if he didn't intend to kill Audrey Ballett you can find him guilty of manslaughter."

The jury went out at 11:55 a.m. Throughout the afternoon they returned several times to have the law explained or to review expert testimony. By 5:45 p.m. a verdict had been reached.

The court room was crowded but silent when Judge Furlong asked, "Gentlemen of the jury, what is your verdict?"

The jury chairman stood and replied, "We find the accused not guilty as charged but guilty of manslaughter."

Judge Furlong: "So say you all, gentlemen of the jury."

"So say we all," responded the jury.

Parsons was asked to stand. Judge Furlong asked, "Do you have anything to say?"

"No," answered Parsons.

Mr. Parsons showed no emotion as the Judge announced a sentence of fourteen years in prison. The maximum penalty was twenty years.

As people in the court room dispersed, defence lawyer Robert Wells told reporters he had no intention of appealing the decision.